2
College Reading

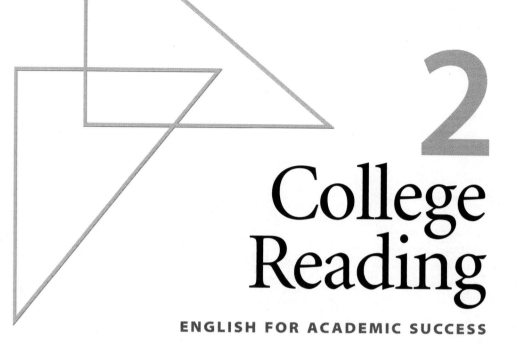

College Reading

2

ENGLISH FOR ACADEMIC SUCCESS

Linda Robinson Fellag

Community College of Philadelphia

SERIES EDITORS

Patricia Byrd
Joy M. Reid
Cynthia M. Schuemann

HEINLE
CENGAGE Learning™

Australia • Brazil • Japan • Korea • Mexico • Singapore • Spain • United Kingdom • United States

HEINLE
CENGAGE Learning™

College Reading: English for Academic Success
Linda Robinson Fellag

Publisher: Patricia A. Coryell

Director of ESL Publishing: Susan Maguire

Senior Development Editor: Kathy Sands Boehmer

Editorial Assistant: Evangeline Bermas

Senior Project Editor: Kathryn Dinovo

Manufacturing Assistant: Karmen Chong

Senior Marketing Manager: Annamarie Rice

Marketing Assistant: Andrew Whitacre

Design/Production: Laurel Technical Services

Cover graphics: LMA Communications, Natick, Massachusetts

Library of Congress Control Number: 2004112210

ISBN-13: 978-0-618-23021-1

ISBN-10: 0-618-23021-1

Heinle
20 Channel Center Street
Boston, MA 02210
USA

Cengage Learning is a leading provider of customized learning solutions with office locations around the globe, including Singapore, the United Kingdom, Australia, Mexico, Brazil, and Japan. Locate your local office at **www.cengage.com/global**

Cengage Learning products are represented in Canada by Nelson Education, Ltd.

Visit Heinle online at **elt.heinle.com**

Visit our corporate website at **www.cengage.com**

Photo Credits: © Strauss/Curtis/Corbis, pg., 1; © Stephane Cardinale/People Avenue/Corbis, p., 3; © Rune Hellestad/Corbis, p. 3; © Feng Shui Institute of America, p. 3; © Lowell Georgia/ Corbis, p. 3; © Michael S. Yamashita/Corbis, p. 7; © Julia Waterlow; Eye-Ubiquitous/Corbis, p. 8; © Bazuki Muhammad/Reuters/Corbis, p. 20; © Nik Wheeler/Corbis, p. 20; © Getty Images, p. 26; © Royalty-Free/Corbis, p. 31; © Japack Company/ Corbis, p. 31; © Royalty-Free/Corbis, p. 31; © Royalty-Free/Corbis, p. 31; © Royalty-Free/Corbis, p. 43; © Nancy Ney/Corbis, p. 43; © Ariel Skelley/ Corbis, p. 48; © Don Cousins, p. 60; © Royalty-Free/Corbis, p. 70; © Royalty-Free/Corbis, p. 82; © Richard T. Nowitz/Corbis, p. 86; © Joe McDonald/ Corbis, p. 100; © Roy Morsch/Corbis, p. 123; © Historical Picture Archive/Corbis, p. 132; © Robert van den Berge/ Corbis Sygma, p. 138; © Royalty-Free/Corbis, p. 145; © Joseph Sohm; ChromoSohm Inc./ Corbis, p. 172; © Archivo Iconografico, S.A./Corbis, p. 190; © Werner Forman/ Corbis, p. 190; © Gianni Dagli Orti/Corbis, p. 190; © Royalty-Free/Corbis, p. 197; © Bettmann/ Corbis, p. 198; © Getty Images/John Crino Collection, p. 199; © Bettmann/Corbis, p. 210; © Corbis Sygma, p. 224; © Robert Nickelsberg, p. 232

Text credits: Acknowledgments appear on page 247, which constitutes an extension of the copyright page.

Printed in the United States of America
10 11 12 13 14 16 15 14 13

Contents

English for Academic Success

English for Academic Success Series

SERIES EDITORS

Patricia Byrd, Joy M. Reid, Cynthia M. Schuemann

▷ What Is the Purpose of This Series?

The English for Academic Success series is a comprehensive program of student and instructor materials. For students, there are four levels of student language proficiency textbooks in three skill areas (oral communication, reading, and writing) and a supplemental vocabulary textbook at each level. For both instructors and students, a useful website supports classroom teaching, learning, and assessment. In addition, for instructors, there are four Essentials of Teaching Academic Language books (*Essentials of Teaching Academic Oral Communication, Essentials of Teaching Academic Reading, Essentials of Teaching Academic Writing,* and *Essentials of Teaching Academic Vocabulary*). These books provide helpful information for instructors who are new to teaching and for experienced instructors who want to reinforce practices or brush up on current teaching strategies.

The fundamental purpose of the series is to prepare students who are not native speakers of English for academic success in U.S. college degree programs. By studying these materials, students in English for Academic Purposes (EAP) programs will gain the academic language skills they need and learn about the nature and expectations of U.S. college courses.

The series is based on considerable prior research as well as our own investigations of students' needs and interests, instructors' needs and desires, and institutional expectations and requirements. For example, our survey research revealed what problems instructors feel they face in their classrooms and what they actually teach; who the students are and what they know and do not know about the "culture" of U.S. colleges; and what types of exams are required for admission at various colleges.

Student Audience

The materials in this series are for college-bound ESL students at U.S. community colleges and undergraduate programs at other institutions. Some of these students are U.S. high school graduates. Some of them are long-term U.S. residents who graduated from a high school before coming to the United States. Others are newer U.S. residents. Still others are more typical international students. All of them need to develop academic language skills and knowledge of ways to be successful in U.S. college degree courses.

All of the books in this series have been created to implement the English for Academic Success competencies. These competencies are based on those developed by ESL instructors and administrators in Florida, California, and Connecticut to be the underlying structure for EAP courses at colleges in those states. These widely respected competencies assure that the materials meet the real world needs of EAP students and instructors.

All of the books focus on . . .

- ► Starting where the students are, building on their strengths and prior knowledge (which is considerable, if not always academically relevant), and helping students self-identify needs and plans to strengthen academic language skills
- ► Academic English, including development of Academic Vocabulary and grammar required by students for academic speaking/listening, reading, and writing
- ► Master Student Skills, including learning style analysis, strategy training, and learning about the "culture" of U.S. colleges, which lead to their becoming successful students in degree courses and degree programs
- ► Topics and readings that represent a variety of academic disciplinary areas so that students learn about the language and content of the social sciences, the hard sciences, education, and business as well as the humanities

All of the books provide . . .

- ► Interesting and valuable content that helps the students develop their knowledge of academic content as well as their language skills and student skills
- ► A wide variety of practical classroom-tested activities that are easy to teach and engage the students

► Assessment tools at the end of each chapter so that instructors have easy-to-implement ways to assess student learning and students have opportunities to assess their own growth

► Websites for the students and for the instructors: the student sites provide additional opportunities to practice reading, writing, listening, vocabulary development, and grammar. The instructor sites provide instructor's manuals, teaching notes and answer keys, value-added materials like handouts and overheads that can be reproduced to use in class, and assessment tools such as additional tests to use beyond the assessment materials in each book.

▷ What Is the Purpose of the Reading Strand?

The four books in the reading strand focus on the development of reading skills and general background knowledge necessary for college study. These books are dedicated to meeting the academic needs of ESL students by teaching them how to handle reading demands and expectations of freshman-level classes. The reading selections come from varied disciplines, reflecting courses with high enrollment patterns at U.S. colleges. The passages have been chosen from authentic academic text sources, and are complemented with practical exercises and activities that enhance the teaching-learning process. Students respond positively to being immersed in content from varied disciplines, and vocabulary and skills that are easily recognized as valuable and applicable.

Because of the importance of academic vocabulary in both written and spoken forms, the reading strand features attention to high-frequency academic words found across disciplines. The books teach students techniques for learning and using new academic vocabulary, both to recognize and understand the words when they read them, and to use important words in their own spoken and written expressions.

In addition to language development, the books provide for content and academic skill development with the inclusion of appropriate academic tasks and by providing strategies to help students better understand and handle what is expected of them in college classes. Chapter objectives specified at the beginning of each chapter include some content area objectives as well as reading and academic skills objectives. For example, student work may include defining key concepts from a reading selection, analyzing the use of facts and examples to support a theory, or paraphrasing information from a reading as they report back on points they have learned. That is, students are not taught to work with the reading selections for some abstract reason, but learn to make a powerful connection between working with the exercises and activities and success with teacher-assigned tasks from general education disciplines. The chapter objectives are tied to the series competencies which were derived from a review of educator-generated course expectations in community college EAP programs and they reflect a commitment to sound pedagogy.

Each book has a broad "behind-the-scenes" theme to provide an element of sustained content. These themes were selected because of their high interest for students; they are also topics commonly explored in introductory college courses and so provide useful background for students. Materials were selected that are academically appropriate but that do not require expert knowledge by the teacher. The following themes are explored in the reading strand—Book 1: Society, Book 2: Enduring Issues, Book 3: Diversity, and Book 4: Memory and Learning.

The series also includes a resource book for teachers called *Essentials of Teaching Academic Reading* by Sharon Seymour and Laura Walsh. This practical book provides strategies and activities for the use of instructors new to the teaching of reading and for experienced instructors who want to reinforce their practices or brush up on current teaching strategies.

The website for each book provides additional teaching activities for instructors and study and practice activities for students. These materials include substantial information on practical classroom-based assessment of academic reading to help teachers with the challenging task of analysis of student learning in this area. And, the teacher support on the series website includes printable handouts, quizzes and overhead transparency forms, as well as teaching tips from the authors.

▷ What Is the Organization of *College Reading 2*?

College Reading 2 prepares intermediate level students for the demands of college-level academic reading. Six chapters of readings in sociology, international studies, psychology, physiology, genetics, literature, women's studies, geology, archaeology, and history present concepts and language that many students will encounter in future courses. The English for Academic Success Reading competencies, as well as academic success, content knowledge, and power grammar activities are logically presented, and then reinforced.

Vocabulary development is a key feature of *College Reading 2*, so each reading selection was analyzed for its Flesch-Kincaid Grade Level, reading ease, and other factors to ensure that readings were appropriate for the intermediate level.

In addition, rather than "grammar in context," *College Reading 2* exploits "grammar from [the] context," of the readings.

Chapter Organization

The chapters are divided into Reading Assignments, each with the following common features to provide prereading, reading, and postreading activities for each reading.

Getting Ready to Read

Schema-building activities—photographs, group discussions, etc.—activate students' prior knowledge before reading.

Reading for a Purpose

In this section, readers are guided to read for specific information through pre-reading tests, prediction of ideas, formation of pre-reading questions, and other tasks.

Reading the Selection This is the actual reading selection, often with a brief introduction.

Assessing Your Learning Following the reading selection, a variety of exercises provide students with an opportunity to interact with what they have read and demonstrate learning. Some of these include:

Demonstrating Comprehension Instead of monotonous comprehension exercises, *College Reading 2* features a variety of interest-peaking activities to monitor comprehension. After each reading, there is not just one or two, but multiple opportunities to assess comprehension.

Questions for Discussion Once students demonstrate a basic understanding of a reading selection, they delve more deeply into its content and language through group and pair discussions as well as individual writing tasks.

Focusing on [discipline area] Here students are exposed to exercise types and activities reflective of the discipline chapter theme.

Reading Journal The reading journal feature also facilitates the reading-writing link. Students express reactions to key ideas in reading or write extended answers to discussion questions.

Linking Concepts In this section, readers synthesize information gained from two or more reading selections and transfer ideas from reading to their experiences.

Learning Vocabulary Each reading unobtrusively marks academic words with dotted underlines and has a footnoted glossary. A variety of practice activities for learning these AWL words appear after each reading.

Assessing Your Learning at the End of a Chapter

Here, students test themselves individually and in groups on their understanding and retention of important content and language features in the readings. Academic vocabulary in the chapter is revisited through a variety of activities.

Acknowledgments

My sincere thanks go to Steve Jones for his discerning "quibbles and bits" of advice. John Pinto, Judy Reitzes, and Michelle Sun, advisor-colleagues, also helped guide this book through its early stages. The following reviewers contributed practical comments:

Marsha Abramovich, Tidewater Community College
Harriet Allison, Gainesville College
Anne Bachmann, Clackamas Community College
Peggy Breedlove, Collin County Community College
Marvelyn Bucky, San Diego State University
Ron Clark, Boston University
Amy Drabek, Queens College
Duffy Galda, Pima Community College
Sally Gearhart, Santa Rosa Community College
Linda Linn, San Jacinto College
Lorraine Segal, Napa Valley College
Alan Shute, Bunker Hill Community College
Lisa Stelle, Northern Virginia Community College
Colleen Weldele, Palomar College

ESL director Susan Maguire made the project a reality, and developmental editor Kathy Sands Boehmer kept our team of educator-writers on track. Series editors Patricia Byrd (Georgia State University), Joy Reid (University of Wyoming), and Cynthia Schuemann (Miami-Dade College), as well as all the team members, lent an enormous store of theoretical and pedagogical knowledge to the series.

Finally, students are the core reason that teachers strive to improve methods and materials. My students at Community College of Philadelphia are especially deserving. Work and family responsibilities, urban, cultural, and language challenges—all of these difficulties impact my students as they work toward their academic goals. Above all, I dedicate these materials to them and wish them success.

▽ **What Student Competencies Are Covered in**
College Reading 2?

Description of Overall Purposes

Students continue to develop academic reading abilities including text on contemporary academic and literary topics with an emphasis on extensive reading and the enhancement of critical reading skills.

Materials in this textbook are designed with the following minimum exit objectives in mind:

Competency 1:
(level/global focus)

The student will read a variety of texts of varying lengths on contemporary academic and literary topics with some fluency and speed emphasizing vocabulary expansion. (High intermediate level, sources include material from Houghton Mifflin secondary textbooks, approximate readability level 8–10.)

Competency 2:
(components)

The student will enhance ability to distinguish between main ideas, such as theories to be learned, and supporting information/details/examples in selected texts.

Competency 3:
(organization)

The student will use a variety of textual clues (e.g., sentence connectors, signal words, and pronoun reference) to understand and discuss the meaning and structure (i.e., patterns of organization) of a text.

Competency 4:
(vocabulary)

The student will develop vocabulary by applying effective strategies to learn the meaning of new words.

Competency 5:
(vocabulary)

The student will enhance development of strategies for discriminating important terminology to be learned for academic purposes such as test-taking, writing, and classroom discussion.

Competency 6:   The student will develop the following critical thinking
(critical thinking)   skills when reading. The student will:
   a. draw plausible conclusions from stated information.
   b. make plausible predictions.
   c. transfer insights gained from readings to other
       contexts (e.g., demonstrating an ability to make
       connections, comparisons, or contrasts).
   d. distinguish scientific fact from opinion.
   e. clarify and analyze the meaning of text (e.g., through
       simple outlining or note-taking and summarizing).
   f. apply content knowledge to academic tasks such as
       solving problem sets, taking tests, or completing
       other work that would be required by an instructor,
       based on subject matter content.

Competency 7:   The student will recognize common cultural references.
(culture)

Competency 8:   The student will enhance English/English dictionary
(dictionary)   skills.

Competency 9:   The student will enhance awareness of study/reading
(study strategies)   skills necessary when reading for academic purposes.

▷ What Are the Features of the Reading Books?

The English for Academic Success series is a comprehensive program of student and instructor materials. The fundamental purpose of the program is to prepare students who are not native speakers of English for academic success in U.S. college degree programs.

The Reading strand of the English for Academic Success series focuses on the development of reading skills and general background knowledge. It is dedicated to meeting the academic needs of students by teaching them how to handle the reading demands and expectations of freshman-level college classes. The four books provide reading selections from authentic academic text sources and practical exercises and activities that enhance the teaching-learning process. Students respond positively to being immersed in vocabulary, content, and skills that are easily recognized as valuable and applicable.

Authentic Academic Reading Selections: The reading selections come from varied disciplines reflecting freshman-level courses with high enrollment patterns at U.S. colleges. The selections represent true reading demands college students face.

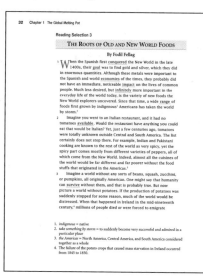

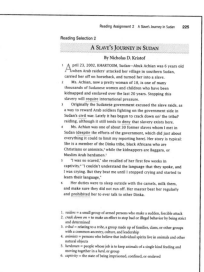

Content and Academic Skill Development: In addition to language development, the books provide for content and academic skill development with the inclusion of appropriate academic tasks and by providing strategies to help students better understand and handle what is expected of them in college classes.

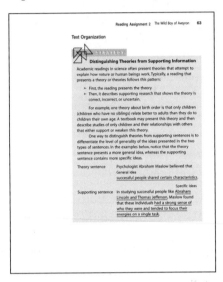

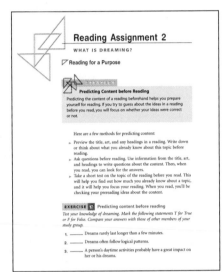

Academic Vocabulary: Academic vocabulary is important in both written and spoken forms, so the reading strand features attention to high-frequency academic words found across disciplines. The books teach students techniques for learning and using new academic vocabulary and provides many practice exercises.

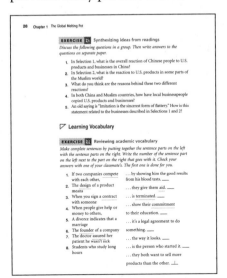

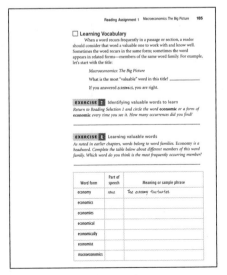

Integrated Review and Assessment: Each chapter closes by revisiting objectives and vocabulary and provides a practice test.

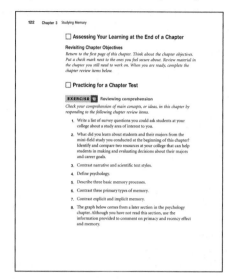

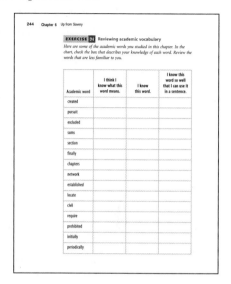

Master Student Tips: Master Student Tips throughout the textbooks provide students with comments on a particular strategy, activity, or practical advice to follow in an academic setting.

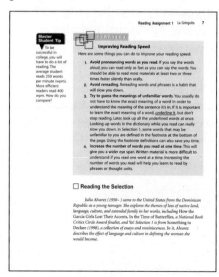

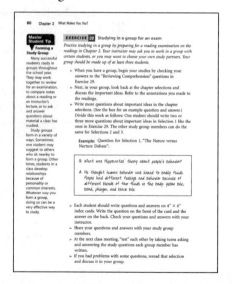

Power Grammar Boxes: Students can be very diverse in their grammar and rhetorical needs so each chapter contains Power Grammar boxes that introduce the grammar structures students need to be fluent and accurate in academic English.

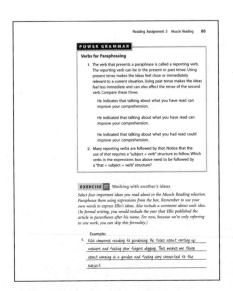

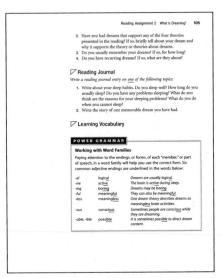

Ancillary Program: The following items are available to accompany the English for Academic Success series Reading strand:

▶ Instructor website: Additional teaching materials, activities, and robust student assessment.

▶ Student website: Additional exercises and activities.

▶ The English for Academic Success series Vocabulary books: You can choose the appropriate level to shrinkwrap with your text.

▶ *The Essentials of Teaching Academic Reading* by Sharon Seymour and Laura Walsh is available for purchase. It gives you theoretical and practical information for teaching reading.

The Global Melting Pot

ACADEMIC FOCUS:
SOCIOLOGY AND INTERNATIONAL STUDIES

Academic Reading Objectives

After completing this chapter, you should be able to:

✓ Check here as you master each objective.

1. Know more vocabulary words used in your academic studies ☐
2. Read academic texts for information ☐
3. Identify a main idea and major points ☐
4. Create an academic vocabulary word list ☐
5. Express your thoughts about ideas in readings by writing in a journal ☐
6. Transfer ideas gained from reading to your personal experience ☐
7. Synthesize ideas from different reading sources ☐

Sociology and International Studies Objectives

1. Know more about topics of study in sociology and international studies ☐
2. Examine your own life from a sociological viewpoint ☐

Reading Assignment 1

BUICKS, STARBUCKS, AND FRIED CHICKEN: STILL CHINA?

▷ Getting Ready to Read

EXERCISE **1** **Participating in class discussion**

Discuss the following questions with your classmates.

1. The word *culture* can be defined as a particular society or group of people and its way of life. Which cultural group or groups do you belong to? What aspects of your life identify you as belonging to one or more cultures? Explain.
2. Which cultural groups can you identify in your college? In your community? What aspects of the people around you identify their cultures?
3. Think about the way you live, spend your free time, eat, dress, travel, or work. In the chart, write things you do, wear, eat, and so on, that represent different cultures. Two examples are provided.

food	Chinese food
clothes	
entertainment	hip-hop music (African American culture)
transportation	
other areas of your life	

EXERCISE 2 **Reading titles and previewing information**

Read the titles of the reading selections below. Think about the selections you will read.

Selection titles

1. "Buicks, Starbucks and Fried Chicken: Still China?"
2. "The Muslim World of Colas"
3. "The Roots of Old and New World Foods"

Discuss the following questions in a group. Take notes on what your group members know. This will help prepare you to read.

1. *Study the items below. How does each item represent more than one culture? If you're unfamiliar with the culture(s) represented by each item, read the explanations at the end of this chapter.*

Shakira

Restaurant sign

Attending a movie premiere

Logos of the Feng Shui Institute of America

Advertisement in Tunisia

2. *List items from* non-Western *cultures that are found in* Western *cultures.*

    _____

    _____

    (Note: Western *countries include the countries of North America and Europe.)*

3. *List items from* Western *cultures that are found in* non-Western *cultures.*

    _____

    _____

4. *List all the names of colas and soft drinks you know. Include the names of soft drinks from different countries.*

    _____

    _____

5. *For each food item below, write the part of the world where you think it originated. If you are unsure about the origin of any food item, write the part of the world you closely associate with this food. (You'll learn more about this in Selection 3.)*

    potato: _____

    tomato: _____

    chocolate: _____

    chewing gum: _____

▷ Reading for a Purpose

STRATEGY

Reading for Information

Reading for information, which includes academic reading, differs from pleasure reading. You may read a novel for fun, but the purpose of academic reading is to *gain*, or get, information. Therefore, you cannot read academic texts quickly or skip over parts as you do when you read for pleasure. You will probably need to reread sentences or sections again so that you understand them well. You may also need to remember important information for examinations or later courses in the same academic *discipline*, or subject.

Here are some techniques to use when you *read for information*. Choose the ones that best suit each reading assignment.

1. Preview the text. *Preview*, or view in advance, the reading title and any subheadings (smaller titles within the reading) or art (photographs, drawings, etc.) that accompany the reading. Read the *glossary*, a list of specialized words and their definitions, if one is provided.

2. Read the text nonstop to get the "big picture." The first time you read, don't use a dictionary. Read without stopping in order to understand the general ideas.

3. Mark the text. The second time, you may want to reread without a dictionary, underlining or circling unfamiliar words or ideas in pencil.

4. Reread the text as many times as necessary. Read the text with a dictionary, writing definitions next to unfamiliar words.

5. Check your comprehension. Discuss the text with classmates or your instructor, and do activities that check your understanding of ideas and words.

6. Review the text. On your own or with study partners, reread the text and ask and answer questions about important ideas and new words, and then reread the text again to check your recall (memory).

EXERCISE 3 **Previewing the text**

Discuss the following questions in a group.

1. What does the title of Selection 1, "Buicks, Starbucks and Fried Chicken: Still China?" suggest about the topic of the reading? What might the main idea be?

2. What does the photograph on page 7 suggest about the *content*, or subject matter, in Selection 1?

3. In Selection 1, notice the *glossary*. Glossed words are marked with small numbers. The definitions for these words appear on the bottom of the page on which the words appear in the reading. Which words do/don't you know? Add unfamiliar words and their definitions to the vocabulary list in your notebook.

4. Quickly scan Selection 1 to note that some words are underlined with dots. Dotted underlines are used to identify important academic vocabulary words. You will study these words after each reading.

▷ Reading for Information

As you read Selection 1, follow the "read for information" steps 2 through 4 on the previous page.

Reading Selection 1

BUICKS, STARBUCKS AND FRIED CHICKEN: STILL CHINA?

By Elisabeth Rosenthal
The New York Times

1   Du Yun maneuvered[1] the large orange shopping cart into PriceSmart's parking lot, where she popped open the trunk of her gray economy Buick and began to fill it with plastic-bagged groceries. "I come here once a week, sometimes twice—it's so convenient," said Ms. Du, a working actress. "There was nothing like this in China in the past."

---

1. *maneuvered* = moved or turned skillfullly

2   In the last two years, Ms. Du and her husband—double income, no kids—have taken out mortgages to buy an apartment as well as the car, a Buick Sail, which they consider economical. Her husband is waiting for the day when they can afford a classier second vehicle—preferably a Jeep.

3   Ms. Du, 29, likes to cook traditional Chinese food, but with her 6-year-old niece visiting, they will probably go to Colonel Sanders KFC this weekend. For anniversaries, she and her husband favor T.G.I. Fridays. "I really like the atmosphere there," she said. Like Du, ordinary people in China's cities have found much common ground[2] with Americans, with the way they live converging[3] rapidly in the marketplace.

An American-style supermarket
in Beijing, China

4   In the last few years, China's major cities have sprouted[4] American stores and restaurants at amazing rates, including Starbucks, PriceSmart, Pizza Hut, McDonald's and Esprit clothing outlets. New housing compounds bear names like Orange County and Manhattan Gardens. A high-end Buick is a popular luxury car, a replacement for last year's Audi.

5   Europeans may be in the habit of viewing every Big Mac as a terrifying sign of American cultural imperialism,[5] but Chinese have mostly welcomed the invasion—indeed they have internalized[6] it.

2. *common ground* = an area of agreement, shared values, or shared opinions
3. *converging* = coming together from different directions
4. *sprouted* = emerged and developed quickly
5. *imperialism* = a political system in which one country increases its authority over other countries
6. *internalized* = made it a part of their attitudes or beliefs

In one recent survey, nearly half of all Chinese children under 12 identified McDonald's as a domestic brand, according to Beijing's Horizon Market Research. Like a seed falling on fertile soil, each new Western chain store seems to generate a group of slightly cheaper domestic clones[7] nearby.

6   "Chinese people these days have a very positive impression of American commercial culture and popular culture," said Victor Yuan, president of Horizon. "American products have been a new approach to bridge the gap between the cultures."

7   Several years back a few press commentaries suggested that China should develop its own fast food products to defeat the intruders.[8] But such views are rarely heard today and the numbers speak for themselves.

A McDonald's restaurant in China

8   There are now 80 McDonald's in Beijing alone, a figure that has accelerated greatly in the past two years. The number of Kentucky Fried Chicken outlets has increased by 100 a year for the last 2 years, to about 600.

7. *clones* = persons or things that copy or closely resemble another
8. *intruders* = persons who enter a building or area where they are not supposed to be

9   Shanghai and Beijing each have more than two dozen Starbucks. Most Chinese never drank coffee until Starbucks came to town in 1999, selling small lattes[9] for over $2. "They go there to impress a friend or because it's a symbol of a new kind of lifestyle," Mr. Yuan said.

10   PriceSmart, which opened its first store here in 1997, now has 18, and plans to have 70 by the end of 2003.

11   "My daughter, who's 16, wants to go to the U.S.," said Gao Fugui, a businessman, "but for me there's no point—I have basically the same life here." Mr. Gao, 45, was piling beer (domestic) and wine (imported) into his brand new sport utility vehicle, with pictures of skiers on the side and fake leopard covers on the seats.

12   "Comparing life 10 years ago to now is like heaven and earth," he said. "The quality of life has improved, the country's improved, even people's ideas have changed." A decade ago no one would have predicted that the leisure tastes of China's emerging urban middle class would have such an American feel. There are hip bars for evening. Mall shopping and miniature golf for day. Ski resorts for winter. Water parks for summer.

13   "I like American products, especially clothes and cosmetics—I really follow the styles," said Jiang Sha, 24, who in a white down jacket and blue turtleneck took a lunch break from her job at an environmental monitoring company. Ms. Jiang said she ate Western fast food many times each week. "Why not? It's simple and fast, suited to my lifestyle."

14   In the 1980s, companies from other Asian countries were in a far better position to enter the huge Chinese market, Mr. Yuan said; they shared a culture and, in the case of Taiwan, a language. But, he said, the Western companies did a far better job of getting to know the rapidly changing tastes of the Chinese consumer, even picking local names with great care. Perhaps the finest example of brilliant naming is Coca-Cola—Ke Kou Ke Le, which sounds quite similar to the product's English name but translates as "really tasty really fun."

9. *lattes* = strong coffee drinks topped with foamy milk

15   Over time, Western products and stores have gained a reputation for high quality and good service, Mr. Yuan said. But he added that in some ways the actual products were beside the point.[10]

16   "The Americans here are selling not just products but a culture," Mr. Yuan said, "and it is a culture that many Chinese want."

17   While the Western chains are thriving, it is often the lightning-fast emergence of Chinese-owned copycat stores[11] that has really spread lifestyle changes to the masses. These stores tend to cater to[12] Chinese who cannot quite afford the imports. Ms. Du, the actress, could now also buy her groceries at the domestic Jing Kelong shopping warehouse that opened just next door to PriceSmart. It is part of a rapidly expanding and appropriately named chain: the "Jing" comes from Beijing and the "Kelong" is pronounced the same as the Chinese word for clone.

From "Buicks, Starbucks and Fried Chicken: Still China?," *The New York Times, Beijing Journal*, February 25, 2002. Copyright © 2002 by The New York Times Co. Reprinted with permission.

---

10. *be beside the point* = to not be important compared to something else
11. *copycat stores* = stores that are copies of other people's stores
12. *cater to* = provide a particular group of people with something they need or want

▷ Assessing Your Learning

STRATEGY

Identifying Main Ideas and Major Points

In academic classes, students are often asked to answer questions like "What is the main idea of the reading?" or "What is the writer's main point?"

How do *you* answer such questions?

▶ The main idea of a reading includes both the *topic* <u>and</u> what the writer says about the topic (the writer's overall opinion, idea, or attitude) about the topic. Your answer should <u>not</u> tell simply what the reading is about.

▶ Also, your main idea answer should tell the writer's idea about the <u>whole</u> reading, not just one part of the reading.

Will you find a *main idea sentence* (or *thesis statement*) in every reading?

▶ Not always. Usually, the main idea is stated in a sentence or sentences in the first paragraphs of a reading.

▶ However, a main idea sentence may not appear at all in the reading. Sometimes the writer does not state the main point directly but expects the reader to understand the main idea from the information provided.

What are *major points* in a reading?

▶ *Major points* in the reading are ideas that are part of the overall main idea. Major points support the main idea by explaining or describing more about it.

▶ A major point is usually stated in a sentence, commonly the first sentence of a paragraph (the *topic sentence*), but sometimes a major point may not be stated directly.

▶ There may be one or more major points per one or more paragraphs.

Demonstrating Comprehension

EXERCISE **4** **Expressing the main idea**

Read the four sentences below. Put a check mark next to the sentence that best expresses the main idea of Selection 1.

_____ **A.** Today's Chinese dislike U.S. products and American-style stores.

_____ **B.** The reading is about shopping in China.

_____ **C.** Many Chinese like to shop at supermarkets.

_____ **D.** American businesses and culture are becoming popular in China.

Next, match each of the sentences above that you did not *choose with one of the following descriptions. Put the letter of the sentence next to the appropriate description. Share your answers with classmates.*

_____ This sentence is too general. It only tells what the reading is about.

_____ This sentence is too specific. It tells only about one idea in the reading.

_____ This sentence could be a main idea sentence, but it's untrue, according to the reading.

EXERCISE **5** **Identifying the main idea sentence**

In a group, answer these questions about the main idea of Selection 1. Share your answers with the rest of your class.

1. Reread the first five paragraphs of the reading. Find and underline one or more sentences that best express the overall main idea of the reading. Does more than one sentence state the main idea?
2. Does the main idea sentence appear in the first paragraph of the reading?
3. Other than the main idea, the writer also includes specific *details* (facts, examples, and descriptions about a topic) in the first five paragraphs of the reading. Underline the sentences and parts of sentences that contain details. How do the details help introduce and explain the main idea?

EXERCISE 6 Identifying major points

Read the pairs of sentences below. In the chart, check the sentence that best expresses the major point (rather than a specific detail) in one or more paragraphs of Selection 1. Compare your answers with your those of your classmates.

¶ 1	____ Du Yun shops at PriceSmart one or two times a week.
	____ Du Yun enjoys shopping at PriceSmart.
¶ 2	____ She and her husband don't have any children.
	____ She and her husband have bought an apartment and a car.
¶ 3	____ People like Du like to eat at American restaurants.
	____ Du likes to cook traditional Chinese food.
¶ 4	____ Buicks are very popular automobiles in China.
	____ Many American businesses have opened in China recently.
¶ 5–6	____ Chinese like American products.
	____ Europeans view American products in a negative way.
¶ 7–10	____ The number of American companies in China is increasing.
	____ A few years ago, Chinese newspaper articles urged China to create its own products to compete with American goods.
¶ 12–13	____ Chinese people like to shop at malls.
	____ Middle-class Chinese like the same free-time activities as Americans.
¶ 14	____ Other Asian countries share cultural ties with China.
	____ In the 1980s, Western companies were able to sell products in China better than other Asian companies.
¶ 17	____ Western stores are doing well in China.
	____ The Chinese have created successful businesses that are like Western businesses.

EXERCISE **7** **Reviewing comprehension**

Read the sentences in the left-hand column of the chart that follows. For each sentence, put a check mark next to the sentence at the right with the same meaning. If necessary, look back at the Selection 1 paragraph in which the sentence appears. Be prepared to explain your answers in detail to your classmates.

1. ...ordinary people in China's cities have found much common ground with Americans, with the way they live converging rapidly in the marketplace. (¶ 3)	____ In China, ordinary people like to meet at the markets. ____ The Chinese lifestyle is becoming more and more similar to the American lifestyle.
2. In the last few years, China's major cities have sprouted American stores and restaurants at amazing rates ... (¶ 4)	____ The number of U.S. businesses in China is growing rapidly. ____ The population in Chinese cities is growing slowly.
3. Europeans may be in the habit of viewing every Big Mac as a terrifying sign of American cultural imperialism, but Chinese have mostly welcomed the invasion. (¶ 5)	____ Unlike Europeans, Chinese people like having American businesses in their country. ____ Europeans are trying to stop American businesses from coming into China.
4. Several years back a few press commentaries suggested that China should develop its own fast food products to defeat the intruders. (¶ 7)	____ In recent years, China has created its own fast-food industry. ____ Journalists said in the past that China should create its own fast-food businesses.
5. A decade ago no one would have predicted that the leisure tastes of China's emerging urban middle class would have such an American feel. (¶ 12)	____ People didn't expect Chinese middle class to enjoy the same things as Americans. ____ The number of middle-class people in China is increasing.
6. While the Western chains are thriving, it is often the lightning-fast emergence of Chinese-owned copycat stores that has really spread lifestyle changes to the masses. (¶ 17)	____ U.S. companies are the main reason that the Chinese way of life has changed. ____ Chinese businesses copied Western businesses, which has resulted in lifestyle changes for many Chinese.

EXERCISE 8 Comparing your reading experience

Discuss the following questions in a group.

1. How many times did you read the selection? Did you read it enough times to understand the main idea and major points?
2. Did you mark the main idea and major points in the reading?
3. What other words or ideas did you mark? How did you mark them (e.g., underlining, highlighting)?
4. What words or ideas were difficult to understand? What did you do to help you remember unfamiliar words?
5. Should you change your reading habits in any way when you read for information? Explain.

▷ Focusing on Sociology and International Studies

The reading selections in Chapter 1 explore topics of study in two academic fields: *sociology* and *international*, or *global*, *studies*.

> **so•ci•ol•o•gy** *n.* the systematic, scientific study of human society
>
> **in•ter•na•tion•al stud•ies** *n.* the study of subjects and issues that concern more than one nation

▷ Questions for Discussion

EXERCISE 9 Participating in group discussion

Discuss the following questions in a group.

1. Imagine you are a *sociologist*. Which society or group of people would you like to study? Why?
2. Which areas of society mentioned in Selection 1 would you like to examine if you were a *sociologist*? Why do these topics interest you?
3. As a sociologist, imagine you are studying a Western culture like the United States, Canada, or Great Britain. What important non-Western influences might you want to examine in the West?
4. Imagine you are studying a non-Western culture like China, India, or Brazil. What important Western influences would you like to study in the non-Western culture?

5. Here are some courses students take when they major in international studies at the University of California's Monterey Institute of International Studies:

International Marketing   Translation and Interpretation
Global Business Management   Japan in the World
Trade Diplomacy Studies   Politics and Policy in Mexico

Which of these courses interest you? Why?

6. Which topics in Selection 1 would be of interest to a student in an International Studies program?

▷ Reading Journal

STRATEGY

A *reading journal* is a notebook in which you write about ideas in your reading. In this class, you will use a reading journal to express your thoughts about what you have read. Putting these thoughts into writing will help you to clarify and remember ideas in your reading.

EXERCISE 10 Beginning a reading journal

Write a one-page entry in a reading journal notebook to answer the following questions: What did you learn from Selection 1 about the influences of different cultures around the world? Did anything that you read about Chinese culture surprise you? Give examples. In your opinion, which cultures have had the greatest influence on the world? Explain.

▷ Learning Vocabulary

Academic Vocabulary

Researchers have found that certain words appear over and over again in academic readings. These same words appear across academic disciplines, from textbooks in sociology and world history to articles on business and computer science, so they are very important to learn and remember. As mentioned earlier, common academic words are marked in the reading selections in this textbook with dotted underlines. You may already know some of these words, but others may be new. You should develop a system for recording new words and definitions so that you can study and remember them. Make learning the unfamiliar academic vocabulary words a priority, and you will not only expand your vocabulary *but also* perform better in academic courses.

EXERCISE **11** Reviewing academic vocabulary

Read this list of academic words from Selection 1. Put a check mark next to the words you already know.

economy/economical	income	vehicle
traditional	major	compound(s)
cultural/culture	internalize(d)	survey
identify(ied)	domestic	research
generate	positive	approach
commentary(ies)	symbol	utility
decade	predict(ed)	emerge(ing)/emergence
urban	styles	job
environmental	monitor(ing)	consumer
similar	expand(ing)	appropriate(ly)

In your notebook, create a list of the academic vocabulary words from the list on page 17 that you do <u>not</u> know. Find and copy the unfamiliar academic words and their definitions. Then write your own sentence using each word or copy a sentence with the word from the reading selection.

Example:

1) monitor = to carefully watch, listen to, or examine something over a period of time

I plan to monitor what I eat to ensure that I don't gain weight.

EXERCISE 12 Reviewing academic vocabulary

Complete each sentence by using one of the academic vocabulary words in the box. Use each word only once. The first one is done for you.

emerged	styles	commentary	economical
culture	expand	vehicle	identify
appropriately	tradition		

GLOBAL INFLUENCES IN THE U.S.

Think about the things that typical Americans use every day, and you can understand what global **(1)** _culture_ means. To begin, waking up in a bed may seem like an American

(2) _____, but the bed itself actually came from the Near

East. Even getting dressed is a multicultural activity, considering

the influence of French and Italian fashions on American clothing

(3) _____. Most Americans drink coffee (which may be

grown in Nicaragua or Colombia) and eat breakfast on china plates,

(4) _____ named because they originated in China. After

breakfast, they may read a **(5)** _____ in the morning

newspaper (printed by a process invented in Germany and on paper

originally made in China). To travel to work, many Americans prefer to drive an (**6**) _____ (**7**) _____ made in

Japan or Korea. On the way, they may listen to music (possibly

performed by a band from Cuba). Interestingly, the typical

American may (**8**) _____ some international

products as U.S. goods, but, in fact, a new global culture has

(**9**) _____. In the 21st century, cultural influences will

continue to (**10**) _____ to nearly every region of the

world, as you can see in the United States.

Source: Adapted from Ellis, D. (2000). *Becoming a Master Student.* Boston: Houghton Mifflin Co.

EXERCISE 13 **Finding synonyms**

For each bold-faced word below, find and circle the synonym next to it. Synonyms are words with the same or almost the same meaning. Compare your answers with your classmates'. The first one is done for you.

1. a pleasant **atmosphere**   (feeling)   idea   time

2. a **terrifying** experience   humorous   fortunate   frightening

3. an **invasion** into a   departure   attack   protection
   country

4. **fertile** soil   productive   dead   dry

5. a **slightly** damaged   noticeably   barely   greatly
   product

6. **defeat** the opposition   conquer   lose   accept

7. **accelerate** the car   slow down   speed up   move

8. an **intruder** in my   visitor   invader   guest
   home

9. a **brilliant** idea   intelligent   boring   foolish

Add any unfamiliar words from above to the academic vocabulary list in your notebook. Write the unfamiliar academic words and their definitions. Then, write your own sentence using each word or copy a sentence with the word from the reading selection.

Reading Assignment 2

THE MUSLIM WORLD OF COLAS

▽ **Reading for a Purpose**

EXERCISE **14** **Previewing the text**

Discuss the following questions in a group.

1. Review the title of Selection 2: "The Muslim World of Colas." What does the title suggest might be the main idea of this reading?
2. What do the photographs below suggest about the *content*, or subject matter, in Selection 2?
3. Read the glossary of vocabulary words marked in the two readings. Which words do/don't you know?

EXERCISE **15** **Reading for information**

As you read Selection 2, follow the reading for information steps 2 through 4 on page 5.

French-based Mecca-Cola

Coca-Cola billboard in Tunisia

Reading Selection 2

THE MUSLIM WORLD OF COLAS

1 In the Muslim world, cola drinks are as popular as ever. Coca-Cola and Pepsi are well-known brands. Moreover, in recent years, several Muslim cola drink companies have emerged[1] to compete with the U.S. beverage giants.

2   Zam-Zam Cola, Mecca-Cola, Qibla-Cola, Star Cola, Arab-Cola, and Cola Turka are gaining popularity in Muslim and other countries worldwide. The three latest entrants[2] in the "cola wars"—Mecca-Cola, Qibla-Cola, and Cola Turka—use politically minded advertisements to urge customers to buy cola drinks marketed by Muslim-owned companies, not American brands.

3   Mecca-Cola's cans and bottles have red-and-white designs similar to Coca-Cola's. But their bottles also promise that 10 percent of its profits will be donated[3] to Palestinian children. And their ads have a strong message: buy local, not U.S. brands: "No more drinking stupid," say Mecca-Cola's ads. "Drink with commitment." Mecca-Cola was started in France in November 2002 by a French businessman of Tunisian origins.

4   Likewise, Pakistani businesswoman Zahida Parveen started Qibla-Cola in Great Britain in January 2003. Her company promises to donate 10 percent of its profits to the charity[4] organization, Islamic Aid.

5   Also in 2003, a new Turkish cola, Cola Turka, was launched in Turkey. *Advertising Age* magazine reported that the company's television ads feature U.S. actor Chevy Chase. The ads show Chase and his family in New York City, drinking Cola Turka.

6   Several Muslim colas get their names from the Islamic religion. Mecca, Saudi Arabia, is the religious capital of the Muslim world. Millions of followers make a pilgrimage[5] to the holy city every year. *Qibla* is the Arabic word for the direction in which Muslims face when praying toward Mecca. Zam-Zam is named after Mecca's Zamzam holy spring water.

1. *emerged* = came out or appeared
2. *entrants* = people who enter a competition
3. *donated* = given as a gift to fund or cause
4. *charity* = an organization that gives money to help people who need it
5. *pilgrimage* = a trip to a holy place for a religious reason

7   The Zam-Zam soft drink company was <u>founded</u> in 1954. For a long time, Zam-Zam was the Iranian partner of Pepsi. Then, the Pepsi <u>contract</u> was <u>terminated</u> after the 1979 <u>Islamic Revolution</u>.[6] In the summer of 2002, sales of Zam-Zam rose in Saudi Arabia during the Saudi boycott[7] of Coke and Pepsi. In the United Arab Emirates, a <u>regional</u> drink called Star Cola saw sales explode in 2003.

8   In May 2003, grocery stores in the Arab-<u>dominated</u> Barbes district of Paris reported strong sales of Mecca-Cola. On French television <u>Channel 5</u>, shoppers said they bought Mecca-Cola because the company gave money to Arab charities.

9   <u>Similarly</u>, British shoppers said in the TV report that they would buy Qibla-Cola rather than Coke or Pepsi to show their opposition to U.S. and British political <u>policies</u>. The United States and Great Britain fought a war to overthrow[8] the government in Iraq. Mecca-Cola responded to the antiwar feelings by handing out free bottles of the drink to antiwar protestors in London in 2003.

10   Tawfik Mathlouthi, <u>founder</u> of Mecca-Cola, said in the French TV report that his company was the first to use politics to sell a beverage. He <u>assured</u> customers that his company had worked hard to ensure product quality since taste was the main reason people <u>purchase</u> a cola again.

11   Still, <u>despite</u> the rising popularity of Muslim colas, Coke and Pepsi will continue to <u>dominate</u> the world's cola markets, according to John Sicher, <u>editor</u> of the <u>publication</u> *Beverage Digest*. "One has to be respectful of any product which represents a political or social protest, but in terms of <u>volume</u> and market share, this will not be a threat to Coca-Cola or Pepsi," he said.

6. *Islamic Revolution* = In 1979, the shah (king) of Iran was overthrown by a revolution of his people. They replaced him with Islamic leaders who ruled the country according to the rules of their religion (Islam).
7. *boycott* = to act together by refusing to buy something, use something, or take part in something as a way of protesting
8. *overthrow* = to remove a leader or goverment from power by force

▷ Assessing Your Learning

Demonstrating Comprehension

EXERCISE **16** **Identifying the main idea**

Reread paragraph 1 of Selection 2. Put a check mark next to the sentence you think best expresses the main idea of the reading.

_____ **A.** In the Muslim world, the popularity of cola drinks is decreasing.

_____ **B.** Coca-Cola and Pepsi are popular cola drinks.

_____ **C.** Many people drink colas in the Muslim world.

_____ **D.** In Muslim countries, new cola drinks are challenging U.S. colas.

Next, match each of the sentences above that you did ___not___ choose with one of the following descriptions. Put the letter of the sentence next to the appropriate description. Share your answers with classmates.

_____ This sentence is too general. It only tells what the reading is about.

_____ This sentence is too specific. It tells only about one idea in the reading.

_____ This sentence could be a main idea sentence, but it's untrue, according to the reading.

EXERCISE 17 Identifying major points

Work with a partner. Read the major point sentences in the chart below. With your partner, write the paragraph number(s) in Selection 2 in which these major points appear. Discuss your answers with your classmates.

	Major points	Paragraph number(s)
1	Three new cola companies are using politics to sell their drinks.	
2	Mecca-Cola ads ask shoppers to think before they buy a cola.	
3	The Qibla-Cola company says it will give money to charity.	
4	Muslim colas get their names from religious items.	
5	Cola Turka started in Turkey.	
6	The oldest Muslim cola company started in Iran.	
7	Shoppers in France and Great Britain buy Muslim colas.	
8	Quality is the most important way to make sure people will buy Mecca-Cola again, the company owner says.	
9	An expert on the cola drink industry says that Coke and Pepsi are still the world's best-selling colas.	

EXERCISE 18 Reviewing comprehension

Check your comprehension by marking the following statements T (true) or F (false), according to the information in Selection 2. Rewrite false statements to make them true. Discuss your answers with your partner.

1. _____ Mecca-Cola is one of the newest cola drinks marketed by Muslim-owned companies.

2. _____ Mecca-Cola's cans look very different from Coca-Cola's.

3. _____ The company that makes Qibla-Cola started in France.

4. _____ Both Mecca-Cola and Qibla-Cola state that they will give money to poor people in Muslim countries.

5. _____ Cola Turka's ads show people drinking the cola in Turkey's capital city, Istanbul.

6. _____ The Cola Turka ads feature an American actor.

7. _____ Zam-Zam is the Arabic name for the direction Muslims face when they pray.

8. _____ Zam-Zam Cola is only sold in Iran.

9. _____ The sales of Star Cola declined in 2003 in the United Arab Emirates.

10. _____ According to a French TV report, some British people were against the war in Iraq.

11. _____ The owner of Mecca-Cola uses political issues to sell his beverage.

12. _____ Coke and Pepsi sales will be greatly affected by the Muslim cola companies.

A product label for Mecca-Cola

▷ Questions for Discussion

EXERCISE 19   Participating in group discussion

Read the product label for Mecca-Cola in the photograph. Discuss the following questions in a group. After your discussion, write answers to the questions in complete sentences on another piece of paper.

1. What is your first reaction to the label?
2. Look at the words used in the label. What messages do the words send?
3. At what group do you think the label is directed? Explain.
4. Look at the design of the label, which uses a red background with white letters. Why do you think the company chose these colors and design?
5. Is this an appropriate way to label a product? Why or why not?

▷ Focusing on Sociology and International Studies

EXERCISE 20 Participating in group discussion

Discuss the following questions in a group.

1. As you read earlier, *sociology* is "the systematic, scientific study of human society." Imagine you were a sociologist. Would you want to study any of the topics listed below and mentioned in Selection 2? Explain.

   Muslims   charities
   beverages   advertisements
   prayer   antiwar protests
   Mecca   Arabs in France

2. Which of the above topics might be discussed in an international studies class? Explain.

▷ Linking Concepts

STRATEGY

Synthesizing Ideas from Different Sources

When you *synthesize* ideas, you put them together in your mind. Synthesizing ideas from more than one reading source helps you critically evaluate the information you read.

The more you read, the more informed you will be about a subject. If you read more than one article about one subject, you can compare the information in all the articles to check whether each source is accurate. For instance, if you read an international studies textbook chapter on the growth of U.S. business in China, this will help confirm the information you found in Reading Selection 1, "Buicks, Starbucks, and Fried Chicken: Still China?"

Successful readers remember information they read in one text—and use it to evaluate the ideas they gain from later reading.

EXERCISE 21 Synthesizing ideas from readings

Discuss the following questions in a group. Then write answers to the questions on separate paper.

1. In Selection 1, what is the overall reaction of Chinese people to U.S. products and businesses in China?
2. In Selection 2, what is the reaction to U.S. products in some parts of the Muslim world?
3. What do you think are the reasons behind these two different reactions?
4. In both China and Muslim countries, how have local businesspeople copied U.S. products and businesses?
5. An old saying is "Imitation is the sincerest form of flattery." How is this statement related to the businesses described in Selections 1 and 2?

▷ Learning Vocabulary

EXERCISE 22 Reviewing academic vocabulary

Make complete sentences by putting together the sentence parts on the left with the sentence parts on the right. Write the number of the sentence part on the left next to the part on the right that goes with it. Check your answers with one of your classmate's. The first one is done for you.

1. If two companies compete with each other,
2. The design of a product means
3. When you sign a contract with someone
4. When people give help or money to others,
5. A divorce indicates that a marriage
6. The founder of a company
7. The doctor assured her patient he wasn't sick
8. Students who study long hours

. . . by showing him the good results from his blood tests. ____

. . . they give them aid. ____

. . . is terminated. ____

. . . show their commitment to their education. ____

. . . it's a legal agreement to do something. ____

. . . the way it looks. ____

. . . is the person who started it. ____

. . . they both want to sell more products than the other. _1_

EXERCISE 23 Reviewing academic vocabulary

Put a check mark next to the academic vocabulary words from Selection 2 that you already know.

aid	assure(d)	channel
commitment	contract	design(s)
despite	dominate/dominated	editor
emerged	ensure	founded/founder
likewise	percent	policies
publication	purchase	regional
responded	revolution	similar/similarly
terminated	volume	

Add unfamiliar words to your academic vocabulary list. For each unfamiliar word, write the word and its definition, and write a sentence using the word.

collocations

EXERCISE 24   Studying words that are often used together

In English, words are often used in combination with other words. Circle the words below that are often used with the bold-faced word from Selections 1 and 2. One or all of the words may be correct. Discuss your answers with your classmates. The first one is done for you.

1. We donate (food).

    (money).

    friends.

2. The businesses are thriving.

    The plants

    The children

3. The man gained a reputation.

    weight.

    a message.

4. The people want to overthrow the store.

    the king.

    the government.

5. Many changes spread through the community.

    businesses

    diseases

6. The government is worried about the rising prices.

    people.

    water.

7. After the results were announced, the team felt defeated.

    the young man

    the mayor

Reading Assignment 3

THE ROOTS OF OLD AND NEW WORLD FOODS

▽ **Getting Ready to Read**

EXERCISE 25 Previewing the text

Discuss the following questions in a group.

1. Study the title of Selection 3: "The Roots of Old and New World Foods." *Roots* means "the origins of a custom or tradition that has continued for a long time." *Old World* means Europe and parts of Asia and Africa, whereas *New World* is a historical term that refers to North, Central, and South America. These terms are used to talk about the time that Europeans (of the Old World) first "discovered" the New World. What does the title of Selection 3 suggest the reading will be about?

2. What ideas do the photographs below give you about the content of Selection 3?

3. Read the glossary of vocabulary words marked in the two readings. Which words do/don't you know? Add unfamiliar words and definitions to the vocabulary list in your notebook.

EXERCISE 26 Reading for information

Read the selection first without a dictionary. Reread it as many times as necessary, marking unfamiliar ideas or words, and then writing definitions of new words next to the text. Later, you can add new words to your vocabulary list.

Corn   Tomatoes   Potatoes   Chili peppers

Reading Selection 3

THE ROOTS OF OLD AND NEW WORLD FOODS

By Fodil Fellag

1   When the Spanish first conquered the New World in the late 1400s, their goal was to find gold and silver, which they did in enormous quantities. Although these metals were important to the Spanish and world economies of the times, they probably did not have an immediate, noticeable impact on the lives of common people. Much less desired, but infinitely more important in the everyday life of the world today, is the variety of new foods the New World explorers uncovered. Since that time, a wide range of foods first grown by indigenous[1] Americans has taken the world by storm.[2]

2   Imagine you went to an Italian restaurant, and it had no tomatoes available. Would the restaurant have anything you could eat that would be Italian? Yet, just a few centuries ago, tomatoes were totally unknown outside Central and South America. The list certainly does not stop there. For example, Indian and Pakistani cooking are known to the rest of the world as very spicy, yet the spicy part comes mostly from different varieties of peppers, all of which come from the New World. Indeed, almost all the cuisines of the world would be far different and far poorer without the food stuffs that originated in the Americas.[3]

3   Imagine a world without any sorts of beans, squash, zucchini, or pumpkins, all originally American. One might say that humanity can survive without them, and that is probably true. But now picture a world without potatoes. If the production of potatoes was suddenly stopped for some reason, much of the world would be distressed. When that happened in Ireland in the mid-nineteenth century,[4] millions of people died or were forced to emigrate

1. *indigenous* = native
2. *take something by storm* = to suddenly become very successful and admired in a particular place
3. *the Americas* = North America, Central America, and South America considered together as a whole
4. The failure of the potato crops that caused mass starvation in Ireland occurred from 1845 to 1850.

because of starvation. Of course, today the result would not be so drastic, but what would European cooking be without potatoes and tomatoes? What would McDonald's and other fast-food restaurants be with no French fries and no ketchup?

4   Other foods that came from the Americas may not be so central to world survival as corn, tomatoes, and potatoes, but imagine the United States without vanilla or peanut butter. Many people in the world would say that chocolate is a necessity to them and that life would certainly be different without it. Chewing gum must not be forgotten either, that basic American institution. It had its beginnings in *chicle*, a natural rubber that some Amerindians[5] chewed long before Europeans "discovered" the New World.

5   Many other foods that originated in the New World are not quite so essential but whose absence would still be felt: pineapples, turkeys, avocados, and sweet potatoes, to name a few.

6   However, the discovery of new foods did not just go one way, from the New to the Old World. The Spanish brought with them some products that have completely changed the native cooking and diet of the Americas. Most modern recipes in Mexican and other Latin American[6] countries could not have existed before the arrival of the Spanish. They introduced Latin Americans to beef, pork, chicken, chicken eggs, rice, onions, garlic, all cheeses, butter, cooking oils, wheat flour, breads, sugar, milk, the frying process itself, plus every kind of alcoholic drink except *pulque*,[7] to mention just a few essential ingredients.

7   Both the New World and the Old World underwent culinary revolutions of unprecedented suddenness in world history. In less than two centuries, they created mixtures of old ingredients and cooking processes and new ones that blended so harmoniously[8] that today the people of both of these regions of the world don't think of their foods as foreign at all.

5. *Amerindians* = American Indians, or Native Americans
6. *Latin American* = a native of a country south of the United States, especially a person who speaks Spanish, Portuguese, or French
7. *pulque* = an alcoholic beverage made in Mexico from juice of the agave, a desert plant related to cactus
8. *harmoniously* = in an agreeable way

▷ Assessing your Learning

Demonstrating Comprehension

EXERCISE 27 Identifying the main idea

Reread paragraph 1 of Selection 3. Underline the two sentences that express the main idea of the whole reading. Share your answer with your classmates.

EXERCISE 28 Reviewing comprehension

Check your comprehension by marking the following statements T (true) or F (false), according to the information in Selection 3. On another sheet of paper, rewrite false statements to make them true. Discuss your answers with your partner's.

1. _____ Explorers came to the New World to find new types of food.

2. _____ Tomatoes originated in Italy.

3. _____ The writer thinks that squash is more important than potatoes.

4. _____ According to the reading, peanuts originally came from the Americas.

5. _____ Old World explorers did not introduce any foods to the New World people.

6. _____ According to the reading, the process of frying food originated in the Old World.

7. _____ The writer thinks the "culinary revolution" he describes happened very slowly over a long time period.

EXERCISE **29** **Scanning for information**

Scanning *a reading means looking it over quickly to find specific information. Scan Selection 3. Look for the names of food items that came from the New World and the Old World. List them in the chart.*

Foods that originated from . . .	
. . . the New World	. . . the Old World

 **Linking Concepts**

STRATEGY

From Reading to Personal Experience

Academic reading can give you more than simply facts. It can help you better understand your own life experiences. For example, a scientific reading about *nutritional values of food* may suggest that a person should eat certain types of food every day. You can transfer the information from a reading on nutrition to your own situation, and you will gain information about your own eating habits.

EXERCISE 30 **Transferring reading ideas to your experience**

Discuss the following questions in a group. After your discussion, write answers to the questions in complete sentences on separate paper.

1. As you recall, *Old World* refers to Europe, Africa, and Asia, and *New World* is a historical term that referred to the Americas—North, Central, and South America and the Caribbean—before they were "discovered" by the Old World. Do you have origins in an Old World country or a New World country? Explain.

2. Which food items that you commonly eat originally come from the New World?

3. Which food items that you often eat come from the Old World?

4. In the community where you now live, how are foods from different cultures blended? Give some examples.

5. Do you think the blending of foods from culture to culture is a negative or a positive thing? Explain.

▷ Reading Journal

EXERCISE 31 **Responding in a reading journal**

Write a one- to two-page reading journal entry on <u>one</u> of the two topics below:

1. Write a journal entry to describe global culture. Would you describe it as a "soup" or a "salad"?

   Some people call the world a "melting pot," where different cultures (the ingredients of the soup) blend together. In the cultural "soup," each "ingredient," or culture, may become so blended with the others that it's no longer an individual item. Others compare global culture to a salad bowl in which many different cultures (ingredients) are "tossed" together in a bowl, but each culture (or ingredient) remains separate.

   In your journal entry, explain why you think global culture should be described as "soup" or "salad." Include your own ideas <u>and</u> some ideas you got from the reading selections in this chapter.

2. Write three "reaction" paragraphs to ideas in the chapter reading selections—one paragraph about one idea in each of the chapter's selections. First, scan Selection 1. Find and underline one interesting idea. On your journal page, write the Selection 1 title: "Buicks, Starbucks and Fried Chicken: Still China?" and copy the sentence(s) you underlined from this reading. Write a paragraph to give your reactions to the idea in the sentence(s). Do the same for Selections 2 and 3. Use the following guiding questions to write your reaction paragraphs:

   ► What does the sentence from the reading mean? Explain it briefly.
   ► Do you agree or disagree with the idea? Explain why or why not.
   ► Do you have any experience or knowledge to support or *contradict* this idea (show that the idea is wrong or not true)? If so, explain it.

▷ Learning Vocabulary

EXERCISE 32 Reviewing academic vocabulary

Find a synonym (a word with the same or almost the same meaning) in Selection 3 for each underlined word in the sentences below. Write the synonyms on the lines below. Check your answers with one of your classmates.

1. When the Spanish first <u>defeated</u> Latin America in the late 1400s, their purpose was to find gold and silver, which they found in <u>huge</u> amounts.

   defeated = _____

   huge = _____

2. Even though these metals were valuable to Spain and other nations, the metals didn't really have an immediate, recognizable <u>effect</u> on the typical person's life.

   effect = _____

3. Much less in demand, but <u>forever</u> more important in everybody's lives today, is the number of new foods the New World explorers discovered.

   forever = _____

4. Imagine a world without beans, squash, zucchini, or pumpkins, all of which originated in the Americas. One might say that people can <u>live</u> without these foods, which is most likely true.

   live = _____

5. Also, we can't forget chewing gum, which is a basic <u>tradition</u> in the United States.

   tradition = _____

6. The foods of both the Old World and New World <u>experienced</u> <u>great changes</u> with <u>unmatched</u> speed.

   experienced = _____

   great changes = _____ (1 word synonym)

   unmatched = _____

7. In no more than two hundred years, they <u>developed</u> mixtures of old and new ingredients and <u>methods</u> of cooking that mixed so well together that today, people of both these <u>areas</u> of the world don't consider their foods to be foreign at all.

   developed = _____

   methods = _____

   areas = _____

EXERCISE 33 **Reviewing academic vocabulary**

Put a check mark next to the academic vocabulary words from the reading selection that you already know.

available	create(d)	economy(ies)
enormous	goal	impact
infinitely	institution	plus
process(es)	range	region(s)
revolution(s)	survival/survive	undergo/underwent
unprecedented		

Add unfamiliar words to your academic vocabulary list. For each unfamiliar word, write the word and its definition, and write a sentence using the word.

POWER GRAMMAR

Adjectives and Adverbs

Adjectives and *adverbs* are words that describe. Adjectives describe nouns (generally names of people, places, and things), and adverbs can describe verbs and adjectives. In the example sentences that follow, notice that adjectives commonly appear before nouns or after *be* and other linking verbs. Adverbs may be used before adjectives or after verbs.

               adverb   adjective noun

Reading is an <u>extremely</u> <u>important</u> <u>skill</u> for students.

                       adverb   adverb   adjective

Therefore, students who read <u>well</u> will be <u>academically</u> <u>successful</u>.

EXERCISE 34 **Working with adjectives and adverbs**

Adjectives and adverbs are underlined in the sentences that follow. Write short answers to the questions to check your comprehension of the underlined words.

1. What is one <u>immediate</u> problem in your life that you need to solve?
             adjective

2. Have you made any <u>noticeable</u> changes to your appearance lately? Explain.   adjective

3. Who is the most <u>essential</u> person in your life?
             adjective

4. What is the most <u>drastic</u> change you have ever experienced in your life?   adjective

5. If you felt very <u>distressed</u> about a problem, whom would you ask for help?   adjective

6. If you feel <u>quite</u> tired, exactly how tired are you?
             adverb

7. How would you describe a family in which the members live <u>harmoniously</u>?
      adverb

▷ **Assessing Your Learning at the End of a Chapter**

Revisiting Chapter Objectives

Return to the first page of this chapter. Think about the chapter objectives. Put a check mark next to the ones you feel secure about. Review material in the chapter you still need to work on. When you are ready, answer the chapter review questions in Exercise 35.

Practicing for a Chapter Test

EXERCISE 35 **Reviewing comprehension**

Check your comprehension of main concepts, or ideas, in this chapter by answering the following questions. First, write notes to answer the questions without looking back at the readings. Then, use the readings to check your answers and revise them, if necessary. Write your final answers in complete sentences on separate paper.

1. How does reading for information differ from pleasure reading?
2. List the six steps to take when reading for information.
3. When you preview a text, what should you look at?
4. The title of Selection 1 is "Buicks, Starbucks and Fried Chicken: Still China?". What is the main point of this reading?
5. When someone asks for the *main idea* of a reading, what information should the answer include?
6. Will you always find a main idea sentence in a reading?
7. What are *major points* in a reading?
8. Why is it important to learn the academic vocabulary words in this textbook?
9. What is happening to the cola drink industry in the Muslim world?
10. Name five foods that originated in the New World.
11. List five common foods that originally came from the Old World.
12. How did New World and Old World originally come together?

EXERCISE 36   Reviewing academic vocabulary

Work with a group of your classmates. Discuss the meanings of the words on <u>one</u> of the lists below. Draw a line through the words on your list that you already know.

Word List A
internalize
survey
generate
emerge
compound

Word List B
monitor
utility
assure
commitment
dominate

Word List C
likewise
revolution
terminate
volume
founder

Word List D
infinitely
institution
undergo
unprecedented
impact

Look up definitions of unfamiliar words in your notebook or in your dictionary. Add the words to the vocabulary list in your notebook, if necessary.

Work with your group members to write a sentence using every word on your list.

After you finish, join another group in your class. Ask the group members to share definitions and sentences for words you do not know.

WEB POWER

Go to **elt.heinle.com/collegereading** to view more readings on global culture, plus exercises that will help you study the Web readings and the academic words in this chapter.

**Explanations of photographs in "Getting Ready to Read,"
Reading Selection 1, Exercise 2**

► Shakira is a rock 'n' roll singer who is popular around the world. She was born in Colombia, her father is Lebanese, and she lives in Miami, Florida. She sings in Spanish, English, and occasionally, Arabic.

► Halal Pizza American Cuisine, the name of a U.S. restaurant, represents several cultures. *Halal* meat means that the animal was slaughtered according to the rules of the Muslim religion. (It is the Islamic equivalent of *kosher* in the Jewish religion.) *Pizza* originated in Italy. The restaurant sign identifies its location as in the United States. And the word *cuisine* is a French word that was adopted into the English language.

► The photograph of American actor Samuel L. Jackson wearing a kilt shows the influences of several cultures, too. The man wears a *kilt*, a traditional skirt worn by men in Scotland. He also wears a Scottish tam, a cap. Jackson is African American.

► The Feng Shui Institute of America indicates the popularity of the Chinese art of *feng shui*, or "the art of placement." *Feng shui* (pronounced fung-shway) attempts to create good relationships between people and the things around them. The fact that this institute exists in the United States illustrates that *feng shui* has become popular all over the world.

► The photograph titled "Advertisement in Tunisia" shows a billboard for Coca-Cola, a U.S. product. The name of the product has been written in Arabic script. This soft drink is sold throughout the world.

What Makes You *You*?

ACADEMIC FOCUS: GENETICS AND PSYCHOLOGY

Academic Reading Objectives

After completing this chapter, you should be able to:

✓ Check here as you master each objective.

1. Know more vocabulary words used in your academic studies ☐
2. Annotate, or mark, important ideas in a text ☐
3. Distinguish between theories and supporting information in readings ☐
4. Recognize multiple meanings of words in dictionaries ☐
5. Recognize word families and their "members" (parts of speech) ☐
6. Form a study group to review for a reading examination ☐

Genetics and Psychology Objectives

1. Know more about genetics and psychology ☐
2. Understand the scientific method ☐

Reading Assignment 1

THE NATURE VERSUS NURTURE DEBATE

▷ Getting Ready to Read

Focus on Genetics and Psychology

The reading selections in Chapter 2 explore topics of study in the academic fields of *genetics* and *psychology*. Study the definitions below:

ge • net • ics *n.*   the branch of biology that deals with the principles of heredity and the variation of inherited characteristics among similar or related living things

gene *n.*   a segment of DNA, located at a particular point on a chromosome, that determines hereditary characteristics

psy • chol • o • gy *n.*   the scientific study of mental processes and behavior

EXERCISE 1   Participating in class discussion

Discuss the following questions with your classmates.

1. Considering the definitions above, what topics of study do you think might interest both *geneticists* and *psychologists*?
2. What <u>physical</u> traits, or characteristics, were passed on to you from your parents?
3. Do you think people are born with their <u>personality</u> or certain ways of behaving? Or you do think people get their personality or behavior from experiences that happen to them after they are born? Explain.
4. Give some examples of qualities and habits you seem to have been born with.
5. Give some examples of qualities and habits you have gained from your experiences.

EXERCISE 2 Reading titles and previewing information

Read over the titles of the reading selections below. Think about the selections you will read.

Selection titles

1. "The Nature versus Nurture Debate"
2. "The Wild Boy of Aveyron"
3. "Mark and John: A Study of Twins"

Discuss the following questions in a group. Take notes on what your group members know. This will help prepare you to read.

1. Both geneticists and psychologists are interested in a person's behavior. They continue to debate about the main source of personality. Some believe that people are born with a certain *nature*. Others believe that personality comes from *nurture*, or how people are fed and protected in an environment, and from their experiences. Which side of the debate do you favor?

_____

_____

_____

2. "The Wild Boy of Aveyron" was discovered in France in the 1700s. What do you know about this story? What can you guess?

_____

_____

_____

3. Why do you think researchers in genetics and *psychology* (the scientific study of mental processes and behavior) study twins? In other words, what do you think they might learn from twins?

_____

_____

_____

▷ Reading for a Purpose

Reading for Information

EXERCISE 3   Previewing the text

Discuss the following questions in a group:

1. What does the photograph on page 48 suggest about the content of Selection 1, "The Nature versus Nurture Debate"?

2. Read the first sentence of Selection 1. What are the two sides of the debate?

3. Now that you have read the first sentence of the reading, which side of the debate does the paragraph on page 48 support? In other words, does the photo suggest that nature, or nurture, affects behavior?

4. Read the subheadings (Hippocrates' Theory, etc.) in Selection 1. What topics do the subheadings suggest?

5. In Selection 1, notice the glossed words marked with small numbers. The definitions for these words appear on the bottom of the page on which the words appear in the reading. Discuss the words and definitions.

6. Selection 1 also contains many academic words (marked with dotted underlines). Scan the reading to find the academic words. Discuss the words and their meanings.

Reading for Information

As you did in Chapter 1, read Selection 1 the first time nonstop to understand the general ideas. Then, reread it as many times as necessary, marking unfamiliar words and writing definitions of new words next to the text.

STRATEGY

Annotating a Text

In Chapter 1, you marked unfamiliar words or ideas in your second reading. When you read academic texts, you read to gain information, so you should also mark, or *annotate*, important ideas. Highlight or underline sentences or phrases that contain important ideas. Don't highlight every sentence and every idea. In addition, to help you locate these important ideas for later study, write a few words about the ideas in the margins of the reading.

Here are some ideas you should highlight and mark in academic reading:

▶ **Key terms in an academic field.** For example, in the fields of genetics and psychology, *genes* is a key term.

▶ **Proper names of people, places, events, and dates.** In every academic field, names of people and what they did, events, and dates are ideas you are expected to remember. For instance, in the field of psychology, *The Wild Boy of Aveyron* is an important name.

▶ **Concepts and theories.** A *concept* is an idea or understanding, based on known facts or observation, of how something is. A *theory* is a set of statements or principles, based on limited information or knowledge, that is designed to explain an event or a group of events and that can be used to make predictions about natural phenomena. In academic readings, you will find explanations of concepts and theories. These ideas are often associated with people or groups of people. For example, in psychology, *Sigmund Freud* believed in the importance of early childhood experiences.

EXERCISE 4 **Annotating the text**

As you read Selection 1 again, highlight or underline lines in the reading that contain important ideas. Look for ideas related to the subheadings. Then, write a few words in the margins of the reading to mark these ideas for later study.

Here's an example of how you might highlight and mark paragraph 1 of Selection 1:

*Debate:
  nature vs. nurture

1 A debate has raged for centuries over what influence on behavior is greater: nature, the personality and genes we're born with, or nurture, the environment and experiences in our lives.

Reading Selection 1

THE NATURE VERSUS NURTURE DEBATE

1   A debate has raged[1] for centuries over what influence on behavior is greater: nature, the personality and genes we're born with, or nurture, the environment and experiences in our lives.

1. *raged* = continued happening with great force or violence

2   Historically, this debate has been framed[2] in terms of nature versus nurture. The discovery of genes is modern, but since the time of the Greek physician Hippocrates (c. 460–377 B.C.),[3] people have understood that we are born with a certain nature. At the turn of the twentieth century, Sigmund Freud[4] introduced his theories on the importance of early child-rearing[5] experiences. These voices who argued that nurture determined our behavior then dominated.[6]

Hippocrates' Theory

3   Hippocrates suggested that the differences among people's thoughts, actions, and feelings were the result of different blends of four basic fluids in the body. Yellow bile[7] was associated with a quick temper. Blood was responsible for a warm, happy temperament.[8] Phlegm[9] produced a cool attitude. Black bile was associated with thoughtfulness or sadness. Physicians at the time focused on balancing these fluids in the body.

Ways to Study Personality

4   Since the time of Hippocrates, psychologists, including Freud, have attempted to describe and explain personality in different types of studies:

  ► In clinical observations, ranging from a psychologist working with a particular problem in a person's life to serious mental illnesses.
  ► In experimental psychology where participants may be observed under a variety of conditions.
  ► Using tests and measurements of various personality factors.[10]

2. *framed* = arranged or organized for a purpose
3. *Hippocrates* = Greek physician who laid the foundations of modern medicine; was known as the "father of medicine."
4. *Freud* = an Austrian psychologist of the late 1800s who believed that early experiences were important for understanding behavior; is known as the founder of psychoanalysis
5. *child-rearing* = child raising
6. *dominated* = had a stronger influence than anything else
7. *bile* = a bitter liquid produced by the liver to help the body digest food
8. *temperament* = the way of thinking, behaving, or reacting typical of a specific person
9. *phlegm* = a thick sticky substance produced in the nose and throat, especially when a person has a cold
10. *factors* = things that influence or help cause a certain result

Major Theories

5   Research has produced five major theories for personality development. One is Freud's psychoanalytical[11] approach. Freud believed that the basic drives of sexuality and aggression[12] and early childhood experiences influenced behavior. His approach focused on the unconscious.[13]

6   A second theory, the trait approach, suggests that personality remains stable over time. Trait theorists believe that social and moral characteristics are relatively unchanging and that they determine our behavior during various situations. Social characteristics include traits such as shyness or sense of humor, and moral characteristics include traits such as honesty or trustworthiness.

7   The behavioral approach claims that there is no need to consider personality or traits because they are created by reinforcement[14] (positive or negative) in the environment. Behaviorist John B. Watson theorized that we behave as we do because early behaviors have been reinforced. Watson claimed that by controlling a person's entire environment from birth, you could make a person into anything you wanted.

8   While behaviorists refuse to look inward and attribute[15] all behaviors to reinforcement from the environment, psychologists who take the humanistic approach emphasize internal positive factors in motivation and personality. Humanist Abraham Maslow focused on an individual's desire to reach his or her full potential. He believed that individuals must find their own paths to that goal, and that successful people share certain characteristics.

11. *psychoanalytical* = relating to the treatment of someone who is mentally ill by talking to the person about her or his past
12. *aggression* = hostile or destructive behaviors or actions
13. *the unconscious* = the part of the mind that contains desires, fears, or memories the person is not aware of and cannot control
14. *reinforcement* = an act of doing something to make an opinion, statement, or feeling stronger
15. *attribute* = to relate something to a certain cause or source

context

9   Other theories about personality have grown in importance and replaced the older theories. These include the social cognitive approach, which focuses on the context, or situation, in which behavior occurs. One important aspect of personality is one's sense of personal control—whether one's life is controlled by the individual or from outside.

Research in Genetics

10   While psychologists have developed theories about personality, geneticists continue to study the role of genetics in the development of personality. Their theory of personality development is called the biological approach. Research over the past several decades has showed that genes specify the way many of our behaviors are generated. It also has been suggested that genes make someone's personality more likely to respond to its environment in certain ways.

11   Genes help to determine how you behave, yet the way you are brought up by your parents, the education you receive, and your life experiences also affect the person you are.

Source: *Introduction to Psychology,* 2001. Evanston, IL: McDougal Littell.

▷ Assessing Your Learning

Demonstrating Comprehension

EXERCISE 5   **Expressing the main idea**

Read the four sentences below. Put a check mark next to the sentence that best expresses the main idea of Selection 1. With your classmates, discuss why you checked this sentence and not the other sentences.

_____   **A.** Scientists have studied and argued about how environment and genes influence a person's behavior.

_____   **B.** The way you are brought up by your parents affects the person you are.

_____   **C.** This reading tells us about human beings.

_____   **D.** Most scientists agree that both nature and nurture affect a person's behavior.

Next, match each of the sentences above that you did <u>not</u> choose with one of the following descriptions. Put the letter of the sentence next to the appropriate description. Share your answers with classmates.

_____ This sentence is too general. It only tells what the reading is about.

_____ This sentence is too specific. It tells only about one idea in the reading.

_____ This sentence could be a main idea sentence, but it's untrue, according to the reading.

EXERCISE 6   **Identifying major points**

Put a check mark next to the sentence that expresses the major point of each paragraph after paragraphs 1–2 (the paragraphs that present the main idea of the reading). Check your answers by looking back at the reading and your annotation. Then, share your answers with a partner.

Paragraph(s)	Major points
3	___ Doctors tried to keep their patients' body fluids in balance. ___ Hippocrates said people act the way they do because of their body fluids.
4	___ Freud was a famous psychologist who studied personality. ___ Psychologists use different methods to study people's behavior.
5	___ Freud's psychoanalytical approach explained personality in terms of basic needs, early experiences, and the unconscious. ___ Freud believed that childhood experiences affected personality.
6	___ The trait approach suggests that behavior changes depending on the situation. ___ The most important point of the trait approach is that one's personality stays the same for a long time.
7	___ Behaviorists believed that a person could become anything he or she wanted to be. ___ According to the behaviorist approach, personality comes from the environment.
8	___ Abraham Maslow was a humanist psychologist. ___ Humanists believe that a person's inner personality determines her or his behavior.
9	___ The social cognitive approach emphasizes the situation where a person's behavior happens. ___ Newer personality theories have replaced older ones.
10	___ Research shows that genes affect people's behavior. ___ Geneticists study how genes determine a person's behavior.
11	___ Your experiences affect your personality. ___ Both your genes and your environment influence your *personality and behavior*

EXERCISE 7 **Comparing your annotated texts**

After you read Selection 1, discuss the following questions in a group:

1. What words or ideas did you highlight or underline? Why?
2. Did you mark the main idea of the reading and its major points?
3. What words did you write in the margins to mark important ideas?
4. Compare your annotations with those of your group members. What did you learn from your group members' annotations?

STRATEGY

Understanding the Scientific Method

In science, any statement made about nature or human beings must be supported by evidence and is very often tested by means of an experiment. The system of testing ideas is called the *scientific method*. Although different scientists work in different ways, all scientific work has some steps in common. Scientists start by asking questions. They form *hypotheses*, or possible answers to their questions, and then they test their hypotheses in a study or experiment. When a hypothesis is supported in a study, scientists are more certain that the hypothesis is right. A set of connected ideas that explain how nature (or human beings) work is called a *theory*.

Scientific Method

Read the chart to understand the steps of the scientific method. Think about the different steps as they relate to Reading Selection 1.

The Scientific Method of Research

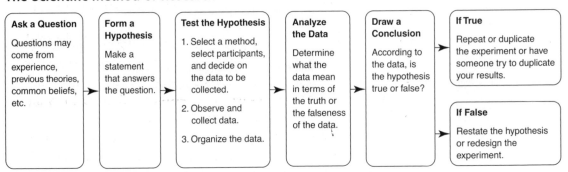

Ask a Question	Form a Hypothesis	Test the Hypothesis	Analyze the Data	Draw a Conclusion	If True
Questions may come from experience, previous theories, common beliefs, etc.	Make a statement that answers the question.	1. Select a method, select participants, and decide on the data to be collected. 2. Observe and collect data. 3. Organize the data.	Determine what the data mean in terms of the truth or the falseness of the data.	According to the data, is the hypothesis true or false?	Repeat or duplicate the experiment or have someone try to duplicate your results.
					If False Restate the hypothesis or redesign the experiment.

Source: *Introduction to Psychology*, 2001. Evanston, IL: McDougal Littell.

▷ Questions for Discussion

EXERCISE 8   **Understanding the scientific method**

Discuss the following questions in a group.

1. Step 1 of the scientific method is to ask a question. What is the central question that scientists are trying to answer in Selection 1?
2. Step 2 is to form a *hypothesis*. A hypothesis is a statement that expresses a scientific "guess" about something in nature. It's a theory that has not yet been proved true or false. In Selection 1, Hippocrates and other scientists formed hypotheses to answer what question?
3. According to Selection 1, what types of tests, or experiments, have psychologists used to test their theories about personality?
4. Which of these ways to study personality do you think is the most useful? Why?
5. Selection 1 reports about theories that have been tested. What is the overall theory that geneticists believe regarding the development of personality?

▷ Linking Concepts

EXERCISE 9   **Transferring reading ideas to your experience**

Discuss the following questions in a group. Then, on separate paper, write an answer to each question. Write in complete sentences.

1. Selection 1 tells us the discovery of *genes* is modern, but for a long time "people have understood that we are born with a certain nature." Think of the brothers and sisters (siblings) in a family you know well. Do the siblings have any personality or behavior traits that they seem to have been born with? Explain.
2. The reading also points out that "the way you are brought up by your parents, the education you receive, and your life experiences also affect the person you are." Think again of the siblings in the family you know. Do they have any personality or behavior traits that are very different from those of their parents? Explain.
3. If you answered yes to question 2, where do you think the siblings got their personality or behavior traits—from their experiences? Their friends? Their education? Explain.

▷ Reading Journal

Write a one-page journal entry in answer to one of the two questions in Exercise 9. Expand the sentences you wrote by giving examples of the personalities and behaviors of the siblings you discussed.

▷ Learning Vocabulary

STRATEGY

Words with Multiple Meanings

In English, one word may have more than one meaning. A dictionary presents the multiple meanings of a word in the order of common use. The number "1" indicates the most common meaning of the word, "2" indicates the second most common meaning, and so forth. When you read, study the words surrounding an unfamiliar word to help you understand which meaning the word has in a particular sentence.

EXERCISE 10   **Choosing meanings from a dictionary**

Study the bold-faced words in the sentences that follow. Circle the appropriate dictionary meaning. (Also note that the dictionary identifies a word by its part of speech (i.e. noun (n), verb (v or vb), adjective (adj), adverb (adv), etc.)

1. A debate has raged for centuries over what influence on behavior is greater: **nature**, the personality and genes we're born with, or nurture, the environment and experiences in our lives.

   nature, *n.* **1.** The physical world and the forces and processes that affect events in it. **2.** The world of living things and the outdoors. 3. The basic characteristics and qualities of a person or thing.

2. Historically, this debate has been **framed** in terms of nature versus nurture.

   frame, *v.* **1.** To build something by putting together structural parts. **2.** To invent evidence to make somebody appear to be guilty. **3.** To arrange or organize for a purpose.

3. These **voices** who argued that nurture determined our behavior then dominated.

> **voice,** *n.* **1.** The sound produced by the vocal organs of a human. **2.** The right or opportunity to express a choice or opinion. **3.** Person, organization, newspaper, etc. that expresses the wishes or opinions of a group of people.

EXERCISE 11 Reviewing academic vocabulary

Review the academic vocabulary words below from Reading Selection 1. Scan the selection to find each word. Reread the sentence in which each word is used.

debate	theories	affect
specify	generated	dominated
environment	decades	respond
research		

Briefly answer each question below.

1. When you have a **debate** about your favorite musical group with a friend, what do you do?

2. When parents **specify** how children should act in a restaurant, what do they tell the children?

3. Describe the **environment** of your classroom.

4. Where do you go when you need to do **research** on a topic?

5. Name one scientific **theory** that was proved to be true.

6. If you **generated** your own electrical power, what could you do with it?

7. For how many **decades** have you been alive?

8. How can your educational **level** affect your life?

9. Name one person who **dominated** you when you were a child. Name another person that *you* **dominated** when you were a child.

10. If someone gives you a present, how do you **respond**?

EXERCISE 12 Reviewing academic vocabulary

Put a check mark next to these academic vocabulary words from Selection 1 that you already know.

debate	negative
environment	attribute, *v*
theory(ies)	emphasize
dominate/dominated	internal
focus(ed)	individual
psychologist(s)	potential
range/ranging	goal
mental	context
participant(s)	occur(s)
factor(s)	role
research	decades
approach	specify
sexuality	generate(d)
trait	respond
reinforcement	affect
positive	

Add unfamiliar words to your academic vocabulary list. For each unfamiliar word, write the word and its definition, and write a sentence using the word.

Reading Assignment 2

THE WILD BOY OF AVEYRON

▷ **Getting Ready to Read**

EXERCISE 13 **Previewing the text**

Discuss the following questions in a group.

1. What does the photograph below suggest about the "wild boy" of Aveyron?
2. Read paragraph 1. How do you think the boy became lost? What do you think happened to him after he was captured?
3. Read the glossary of vocabulary words marked in Selection 2. Discuss the words and definitions.

Reading for Information

As you did with Selection 1, read Selection 2 once without a dictionary. Then, read it again, marking important ideas with a highlighter pen or by underlining, and write words in the margins about these ideas.

Here's an example of how you might highlight and mark paragraph 1 of Selection 2:

*Wild boy,
France, 1700s

1 Reported sightings of a wild boy running naked in the Caune Words of Aveyron, France, caused a stir in the late 1700s.

A statue of the "wild boy" in San Sernin, France

Reading Selection 2

THE WILD BOY OF AVEYRON

1 Reported sightings of a wild boy running naked in the Caune Woods of Aveyron, France, caused a stir[1] in the late 1700s. Supposedly, the boy had been lost or abandoned by his parents at a very early age and had grown up with animals. Eventually this Wild Boy of Aveyron was captured by hunters and sent to Paris. He appeared to be about eleven at the time.

2 In Paris, scientists expected to observe what philosopher Jean-Jacques Rousseau[2] had called the "noble savage".[3] After all, here was a human being who had grown up untouched by the evils of society. But what scientists found instead was a frightened creature who moved like a wild animal and ate garbage. He spent most of his time silently rocking but would snarl[4] and attack anyone who tried to touch him. Although the scientists worked with the boy for over ten years, he never learned to speak. He was never able to live unguarded among other people.

1. *caused a stir* = created a strong feeling of excitement or anger, felt by many people
2. *Rousseau* = a Swiss philosopher, wrote in the late 1700s that humans who lived in natural places were good and admirable. He also said that the individual is essentially good but is usually corrupted by society.
3. *noble* = morally good or generous in a way that should be admired *savage:* an insulting word for someone from a country where the way of living seems simple and undeveloped
4. *snarl* = to make a low angry sound and show one's teeth

3   Could psychologists have "cured" this Wild Boy? Probably not. In more recent times, children have been rescued from years of confinement[5] in closets and other environments that have cut them off from human contact. Without exception, these children have found it extremely difficult to learn language and to interact[6] with others. Cases like these highlight[7] the importance of early contacts with other people for normal human development. They underscore the need to know as much as possible about early development and what can help or hinder it. And they bear on[8] the *nature-nurture* question. Specifically, to what extent is development a product of what we arrive with at birth—our inherited biological nature. To what extent[9] is development a product of what the world provides— the nurture of the environment?

From *Essentials of Psychology*, by D. A. Bernstein and P. W. Nash. Copyright © 2001 Houghton Mifflin Company. Reprinted with permission.

5. *confinement* = the act of making someone stay in a room or area
6. *interact* = to talk to other people and work together with them
7. *highlight* = to emphasize something
8. *bear on* = to apply or have a connection to something
9. *extent* = the limit, size, or degree of something

▷ **Assessing Your learning**

Demonstrating Comprehension

EXERCISE 14 **Identifying main ideas and major points**

Work with a partner to complete the following sentences, which express the main idea and major points of Selection 2, "The Wild Boy of Aveyron." Do this <u>without</u> *looking back at the text. Then, check your answers by scanning for the information in the text.*

The Wild Boy of Aveyron

The wild boy of Aveyron was called "wild" because he grew up

_____. When scientists found him, the

boy acted like _____. However,

scientists had expected the boy to be what the French philosopher

Rousseau called "a noble savage." Rousseau's idea was that someone who

lived in nature should be a person _____.

In the end, the French scientists were not able to teach the wild boy

to _____ .

More recently, scientists have found other children like the wild

boy, who _____. These cases, like the boy of

Aveyron, show the importance of _____

in a person's development.

EXERCISE 15 **Comparing your annotated text**

After you read, compare your annotations with those of a group of classmates. Discuss why you marked certain ideas. Make any additional annotations you think are useful.

Text Organization

STRATEGY

Distinguishing Theories from Supporting Information

Academic readings in science often present theories that attempt to explain how nature or human beings work. Typically, a reading that presents a theory or theories follows this pattern:

► First, the reading presents the theory.
► Then, it describes supporting research that shows the theory is correct, incorrect, or uncertain.

For example, one theory about birth order is that only children (children who have no siblings) relate better to adults than they do to children their own age. A textbook may present this theory and then describe studies of only children and their relationships with others that either support or weaken this theory.

One way to distinguish theories from supporting sentences is to differentiate the level of generality of the ideas presented in the two types of sentences. In the examples below, notice that the theory sentence presents a more general idea, whereas the supporting sentence contains more specific ideas.

Theory sentence   Psychologist Abraham Maslow believed that
                      General idea
                      <u>successful people shared certain characteristics.</u>

                                                            Specific ideas
Supporting sentence   In studying successful people like <u>Abraham
                      Lincoln and Thomas Jefferson</u>, Maslow found
                      that these individuals <u>had a strong sense of
                      who they were and tended to focus their
                      energies on a single task.</u>

EXERCISE 16   Identifying theories and support

Reread paragraph 2 of Selection 2, "The Wild Boy of Aveyron," reprinted below. Notice that the theory *sentences and the* support *sentences have been marked. With a group of your classmates, discuss the level of generality of ideas that distinguish theory sentences from support sentences. Share your ideas with the rest of your class.*

Theory sentence

In Paris, scientists expected to observe what philosopher
Jean-Jacques Rousseau had called the "noble savage."

Support sentences

After all, here was a human being who had grown up untouched by the evils of society. But what scientists found instead was a frightened creature who moved like a wild animal and ate garbage. He spent most of his time silently rocking but would snarl and attack anyone who tried to touch him. Although the scientists worked with the boy for over ten years, he never learned to speak. He was never able to live unguarded among other people.

Next, reread paragraph 3 in the Selection 2. With your group members, discuss three sentences from paragraph 3, reprinted below. Put a check mark in the appropriate place to indicate if a sentence presents a theory or supporting information. Share your answers with the rest of your class.

1. Cases like these highlight the importance of early contacts with other people for normal human development.	—— Theory? —— Support?
2. Specifically, to what extent is development a product of what we arrive with at birth—our inherited biological nature.	—— Theory? —— Support?
3. To what extent is development a product of what the world provides—the nurture of the environment?	—— Theory? —— Support?

▷ Questions for Discussion

EXERCISE 17 **Thinking about the reading**

Discuss the following questions in a group.

1. When scientists first captured the wild boy, the boy ran away. Why do you think he did this? How do you think he felt?
2. The scientists who studied the boy have been criticized for taking him from his "natural home." Do you believe they should have left him in his wild home? Explain your opinion.
3. What do you think scientists could learn from the wild boy?

▷ Reading Journal

Write a one-page journal entry in answer to one of the questions in Exercise 17. Expand the sentences you wrote by giving more details and reasons to support your opinions. Use information you learned from reading Selection 2, "The Wild Boy of Aveyron," as well as your own experience and knowledge.

Here is an example of a reading journal entry:

Reading Journal, Question 1.

The wild boy probably ran away because he felt scared. He had been living like a wild animal in the forest. Maybe he had never seen a human before, or perhaps he knew that humans used guns to kill animals . . .

▷ Learning Vocabulary

EXERCISE 18 **Reviewing academic vocabulary**

Review the list of academic vocabulary words from Selection 2. Scan the selection to find each word, and read the sentence in which it appears.

abandoned	eventually	philosopher	psychologists
contact	interact	highlight	specifically

Which of the academic vocabulary words has the same meaning as the words or phrases below? Write the academic word on the appropriate line.

1. _____ to communicate and work with others

2. _____ to show the importance of something

3. _____ a person who studies what it means to exist

4. _____ exactly

5. _____ left someone or something you are responsible for

6. _____ communication with a person, organization, etc.

7. _____ later, after time

8. _____ people who study the mind and how it works

EXERCISE 19 **Reviewing academic vocabulary**

Put a check mark next to the academic vocabulary words from Selection 2 that you already know.

abandon(ed)	eventually	philosopher	specifically
psychologist(s)	contact(s)	environment(s)	
interact	highlight	normal	

Add unfamiliar words to your academic vocabulary list. For each unfamiliar word, write the word and its definition, and write a sentence using the word.

EXERCISE 20 Choosing meanings from a dictionary

Study the bold-faced words in the sentences below. Circle the appropriate dictionary meaning.

1. **Cases** like these **highlight** the importance of early contacts with other people for normal human development.

   case, *n.* **1.** An instance or example of something. **2.** A legal action; a lawsuit. **3.** A situation that requires investigation, especially by police. **4.** A set of reasons or arguments that support one side of an argument. **5.** A container for storing something.

   highlight, *v.* **1.** To emphasize something. **2.** To mark important passages of text with a marker for later reference.

2. And they **bear** on the *nature-nurture* question.

   bear, *v.* **1.** To have responsibility for something. **2.** To have or show a particular mark, name, etc. **3.** To be similar to something, or to be related to someone or something in some way. **4.** To hold up or support. **5.** To turn right or left. **6.** To give birth to. **7.** To carry or transport somebody or something.

STRATEGY

Word Families and Parts of Speech

Words belong to families. Each word family "member" has a closely related meaning but a different form, or ending. Word families may have *noun, verb, adjective,* and/or *adverb* "members." *Nouns, verbs, adjectives,* and *adverbs* are called "parts of speech." Recognizing word families and the different forms of their parts of speech helps you choose the correct word when you write or speak.

Study how different "members" of one word family are used in the sentences below. Discuss the questions in your class.

In what ways do you <u>interact</u> with your classmates?

Have you had any <u>interactions</u> with your instructor outside of class?

What <u>interactive</u> games or sports do you enjoy?

EXERCISE 21   **Working with parts of speech**

The chart below contains members (parts of speech) of word families. Words from Selections 1 and 2 are printed in bold-faced type. Use a dictionary to find other parts of speech of the same family. Some families have more than one part of speech, such as more than one noun, *and none of another part of speech, such as the* verb. *If a word family does not have a particular part of speech, put a dash mark in the appropriate box in the chart. Compare your answers in a group. The first word family is completed for you.*

Noun(s)	Verb(s)	Adjective(s)	Adverb(s)
abandonment	abandon	abandoned	————
psychologist			
	interact		
			eventually
contact			
	highlight		
		mental	
research			
		normal	
environment			
	respond		

EXERCISE 22   **Using parts of speech correctly**

Fill in each blank with the correct form of the word given. Use a dictionary to help you. Be sure to use correct verb endings. Compare your answers with those of your classmates. The first has been done for you as an example.

The Story of "Genie"

Another true story of an abandon _ed_ child is the story of "Genie." As a young girl, Genie (not her real name) was locked in a room in her parents' Los Angeles suburban home for ten years. Her story was told in a 1997 Public Broadcasting System (PBS) film called *Secret of the Wild Child.* The film highlight_____ the important events in Genie's life.

Apparently, Genie's father thought she was mental_____ retarded when she was born. Therefore, he convinced his wife that they should keep the girl locked in a room. Genie's parents left food for her while she was asleep, but they had no interact_____ with her.

Officials discovered Genie's situation when she was thirteen. They put her parents in jail, and Genie was put into government care. Using research money, scientists began to study Genie. A psycholog_____ named James Kent observed that Genie explored her environ_____ by touching everything and everyone. Unlike the wild boy of Aveyron, Genie eventual_____ learned to say a few words and understand language. In one year, linguist Susan Curtiss helped Genie learn one hundred words. However, psycholog_____ tests showed that she was mental_____ retarded. Research_____ were uncertain whether Genie was born with mental_____ problems or became ill because she had lived so long without human contact.

Genie was still living in government adult care homes when the PBS film was made in 1997.

Reading Assignment 3

LINKING PSYCHOLOGY AND GENETICS

▽ **Getting Ready to Read**

EXERCISE 23 **Previewing the text**

Discuss the following questions in a group:

1. What does the photograph below suggest about this selection?
2. Read the first sentence of the selection. What does this sentence mean?
3. Read the glossary of vocabulary words marked in Selection 3. Discuss the words and definitions.

Identical twins

Reading Selection 3

LINKING PSYCHOLOGY AND GENETICS

1   Mark and John were identical twins separated at birth. The separation occurred because their parents were unmarried and poor. They offered the children to an immigrant couple, but the couple could care for only one of the twins. John grew up with them, secure, and loved. Mark went from orphanage[1] to foster home[2] to hospital and, finally, back to his natural father's second wife. The boys' environments had been completely different, yet their genes were the same.

2   They met for the first time at twenty-four years of age. They are physically alike. The same teeth are giving them toothaches. There are also similarities in their behavior and mental processes. They use the same aftershave,[3] smoke the same brand of cigarettes, brush with the same imported brand of toothpaste, and like the same sports. Both had served in the military and had joined within eight days of each other. IQ[4] testing by a psychologist found they had practically identical overall IQ scores.

3   Our genes and our environment blend together to shape behavior and mental processes. Genetic inheritance is often called our biological *nature*. The environmental conditions and events before and after birth are referred to as *nurture*. Exploring the influences of nature and nurture in relation to personality, mental ability, mental disorders, and other subjects has taken psychologists into the field of *behavioral genetics*. Most behavioral tendencies can be influenced by many different genes, but also by the environment. Researchers in behavioral genetics explore the *relative roles* of genetic and environmental factors in creating differences among behavioral tendencies in *groups* of people.

1. *orphanage* = a public institution for the care and protection of children without parents
2. *foster home* = a household in which an orphaned, neglected, or delinquent child is placed temporarily for care
3. *aftershave* = a pleasant-smelling liquid that a man puts on his face after shaving
4. *IQ* = intelligence quotient; the level of someone's intelligence, with 100 being the average level

4   Research on behavioral genetics in humans must be interpreted[5] with great care. First, environmental influences have an enormous impact on human behavior. Second, legal, moral,[6] and ethical [7] considerations prohibit selective breeding,[8] so research in human behavioral genetics depends on studies in which control is imperfect. Some of the most important research designs are family studies, twin studies, and adoption studies.

5   In *family studies*, researchers look at whether close family relatives are more likely than distant ones to show similarities in behavior and mental processes. *Twin studies* explore the nature-nurture mix by comparing similarities seen in identical twins with those of nonidentical twins. Twins usually share the same environment and may also be treated very much the same by parents and others. So, if identical twins—whose genes are the same—are more alike on some characteristics than nonidentical twins (whose genes are no more similar than those of other siblings), the characteristic may be affected by genes.

6   *Adoption studies* take advantage of the naturally occurring "experiments" that occur when babies are adopted. The logic of these studies is that if adopted children's characteristics are more like those of their biological parents than those of their adoptive parents, genetics probably plays a clear role in those characteristics. In fact, the personalities of young adults who were adopted at birth tend to be more like those of their biological parents than those of their adoptive parents. Especially valuable are adoption studies of identical twins who, like Mark and John, were separated soon after birth. If identical twins show similar characteristics after years of living in very different environments, the role of heredity[9] in those characteristics is highlighted. Adoption studies of intelligence tend to support the role of genetics in mental ability. However, environmental influences are important, too.

5. *interpreted* = explained or decided on the meaning of an event, statement, etc.
6. *moral* = relating to the principles of what is right and wrong, and the difference between good and evil
7. *ethical* = following accepted standards of behavior or conduct
8. *selective breeding:* the act of carefully choosing which animals or plants to mate and produce offspring
9. *heredity* = the passing of traits or characteristics from parents to offspring by genes

Remember that behavioral genetics research looks at the relative roles of heredity and environment that underlie group differences. It cannot determine the degree to which a *particular* person's behavior is due to heredity or environment.

From *Essentials of Psycohology*, by D. A. Bernstein and P. W. Nash. Copyright © 2001 Houghton Mifflin Company. Reprinted with permission.

▷ Assessing Your Learning

Demonstrating Comprehension

EXERCISE 24   **Expressing the main idea**

What is the main idea or point of Selection 3? On the lines below, write a complete sentence to express the main idea. Remember that the main idea sentence should tell the topic *(or general idea) of the reading* and *the writer's opinion, attitude, or idea about the topic. Compare your main idea sentences in your group. Work together to put your group's ideas into one sentence that best expresses the main idea.*

_____

_____

_____

_____

_____

_____

Work with a partner to answer the following questions. First, answer the questions <u>without</u> looking back at the reading. Then, check your answers by rereading the selection. Write the paragraph number where you checked the answer. Share your answers with the rest of the class.

First, answer . . .	Then, check . . .
1. Why were the twins separated?	¶ _____
2. What happened to each twin? Explain each story briefly.	¶ _____
3. What are <u>five</u> similarities between Mark and John? ▶ _____ ▶ _____ ▶ _____ ▶ _____ ▶ _____	¶ _____
4. What is "our biological *nature*"?	¶ _____
5. What is *nurture*?	¶ _____

6. What are <u>two</u> problems about genetics research in humans?

¶ _____

► _____

_____

_____

► _____

_____

_____

7. What do scientists look for when they do the following types of research studies:

¶ _____ and

¶ _____

► *family studies?* _____

_____

► *twin studies?* _____

_____

► *adoption studies?* _____

_____

8. How are *identical* twins different from *nonidentical* twins?

¶ _____

9. Do genetics researchers study how <u>an individual person's</u> behavior changes because of genes or environment? If not, whose behavior do they study?

¶ _____

EXERCISE 26   Identifying theories and support

Selection 3, "Linking Psychology and Genetics," presents two theories and supporting information. Study the theory and support sentences marked in paragraphs 2 and 3, reprinted below. With a group of your classmates, discuss the ideas in each type of sentence.

2 They met for the first time at twenty-four years of age. They are physically alike. The same teeth are giving them toothaches. There are also similarities in their behavior and mental processes. They use the same aftershave, smoke the same brand of cigarettes, brush with the same imported brand of toothpaste, and like the same sports. Both had served in the military and had joined within eight days of each other. IQ testing by a psychologist found they had practically identical overall IQ scores.	Support
3 Our genes and our environment blend together to shape behavior and mental processes. Genetic inheritance is often called our biological *nature.* The environmental conditions and events before and after birth are referred to as *nurture.* Exploring the influences of nature and nurture in relation to personality, mental ability, mental disorders, and other subjects has taken psychologists into the field of *behavioral genetics.* Most behavioral tendencies can be influenced by many different genes, but also by the environment. Researchers in behavioral genetics explore the *relative roles* of genetic and environmental factors in creating differences among behavioral tendencies in *groups* of people.	Theory Theory

Next, work in your group to identify theory and support sentences in paragraph 6 of the selection, printed below. For each underlined sentence, put a check mark next to "Theory" or "Support" to identify which type of information the sentence presents. Share your answers with the rest of your class.

6 *Adoption studies* take advantage of the naturally occurring "experiments" that occur when babies are adopted. The logic of these studies is that if adopted children's characteristics are more like those of their biological parents than those of their adoptive parents, genetics probably plays a clear role in those characteristics. In fact, the personalities of young adults who were adopted at birth tend to be more like those of their biological parents than those of their adoptive parents. Especially valuable are adoption studies of identical twins who, like Mark and John, were separated soon after birth. If identical twins show similar characteristics after years of living in very different environments, the role of heredity in those characteristics is highlighted. Adoption studies of intelligence tend to support the role of genetics in mental ability. However, environmental influences are important, too.	__ Theory? __ Support? __ Theory? __ Support? __ Theory? __ Support?

▷ Linking Concepts

EXERCISE 27 **Comparing a reading to personal experience**

Discuss the following questions in a group:

1. Do you know any twins? If so, do they exhibit similar behavior?
2. If you have siblings, do you and your sibling(s) have the same habits or personality traits? Explain. If you do not have siblings, think of someone you know. Does that person have the same habits or personality traits as her or his sibling or siblings? Explain.
3. Which of the similar habits or behaviors described in paragraph 2 of Selection 3 remind you of habits you share with another person? Is this person your sibling or a friend? Why do you think you share these characteristics?

▷ Learning Vocabulary

EXERCISE 28 Reviewing academic vocabulary

Use the words in the box to complete the sentences below.

identical	secure	processes	overall
occurred	mental	military	underlie
ethical	logic	interpret	role

1. IQ tests measure a person's _____ abilities.

2. In the scientific method, researchers collect data and then _____ it in order to make a conclusion.

3. Scientists want to find out if environmental influences _____ differences in people's behavior.

4. Having a _____ home life can positively influence a child's development.

5. A psychologist studies the _____ of the mind.

6. Researchers find that _____ twins often have the same habits.

7. The _____ behind studying twins who were separated at birth is that they should share characteristics and mental ability.

8. There are _____ concerns about conducting research with animals.

9. The case of "the wild boy of Aveyron" _____ in the late 1700s in France.

10. A career in the _____ requires a person to be physically fit.

11. The _____ conclusion you may make from Selection 3 is that genes influence human behavior.

12. Heredity and environment both play important _____ in developing a person's personality.

▷ Assessing Your Learning at the End of a Chapter

Revisiting Chapter Objectives

Return to the first page of this chapter. Think about the chapter objectives. Put a check mark next to the ones you feel secure about. Review material in the chapter you still need to work on. When you are ready, answer the chapter review questions in Exercise 29.

▷ Practicing for a Chapter Test

EXERCISE 29 Reviewing comprehension

Check your comprehension of main concepts in this chapter by answering the following chapter review questions. First, write notes to answer the questions <u>without</u> looking back at the readings. Then, use the readings to check your answers and revise them, if necessary. Write your final answers in <u>complete sentences</u> on separate paper.

1. What do psychologists mean when they say our behavior is affected by *nature*?
2. What do they mean when they say our behavior is affected by *nurture*?
3. What topics were of interest to Sigmund Freud, who developed the psychoanalytical approach to explain personality?
4. According to the trait approach, what is the most important determiner of people's personality?
5. What did the research of humanist Abraham Maslow focus on?
6. List as many steps of the scientific method as you can remember.
7. Who was "the wild boy of Aveyron"?
8. What did scientists try to do with the boy? Did their efforts succeed?
9. In Selection 3, what do studies of twins such as Mark and John tell us about personality development?
10. What is the difference between *identical* and *nonidentical* twins?

Master Student Tip

Forming a Study Group

Many successful students study in groups throughout the school year. They may work together to review for an examination, to compare notes about a reading or an instructor's lecture, or to ask and answer questions about material a class has studied.

Study groups form in a variety of ways. Sometimes one student may suggest to others who sit nearby to form a group. Other times, students in a class develop relationships because of personality or common interests. Whatever way you form a group, doing so can be a very effective way to study.

EXERCISE **30** **Studying in a group for an exam**

Practice studying in a group by preparing for a reading examination on the readings in Chapter 2. Your instructor may ask you to work in a group with certain students, or you may want to choose your own study partners. Your group should be made up of at least three students.

► When you have a group, begin your studies by checking your answers to the "Reviewing Comprehension" questions in Exercise 29.

► Next, in your group, look back at the chapter selections and discuss the important ideas. Refer to the annotations you made to the readings.

► Write more questions about important ideas in the chapter selections. (See the box for an example question and answer.) Divide this work as follows: One student should write two or three more questions about important ideas in Selection 1 like the ones in Exercise 29. The other study group members can do the same for Selections 2 and 3.

Example: Question for Selection 1, "The Nature versus Nurture Debate":

Q: What was Hippocrates' theory about people's behavior?

A: He thought human behavior was linked to bodily fluids. People had different feelings and behavior because of different blends of four fluids in the body: yellow bile, blood, phlegm, and black bile.

► Each student should write questions and answers on 4" × 6" index cards. Write the question on the front of the card and the answer on the back. Check your questions and answers with your instructor.

► Share your questions and answers with your study group members.

► At the next class meeting, "test" each other by taking turns asking and answering the study questions each group member has written.

► If you had problems with some questions, reread that selection and discuss it in your group.

EXERCISE 31 **Reviewing academic vocabulary**

In your study group, discuss the following academic words from the chapter selections. Scan the reading selections to find each word. Read the sentence in which the word was used so that you can better understand its meaning.

debate	abandoned	identical
eventually	occurred	generated
dominated	psychologists	secure

As a group, review the definitions and sentences of the words you wrote for your academic vocabulary list.

▶ Divide the words equally among your group members. For each of your words, copy a sentence with a blank space for the academic word.

▶ Test each other on the academic vocabulary words by sharing your sentences. Ask your group members to take turns filling in the blanks.

WEB POWER

Go to elt.heinle.com/collegereading to view more readings on the nature versus nurture debate, plus exercises that will help you study the Web readings and the academic words in this chapter.

To Sleep, To Dream

ACADEMIC FOCUS: PHYSIOLOGY AND PSYCHOLOGY

Academic Reading Objectives

After completing this chapter, you should be able to:

✓ Check here as you master each objective.

1. Know more vocabulary words used in your academic studies ☐
2. Recognize and produce a text with a series of actions that someone does to get a particular result (a process text) ☐
3. Identify details in a reading ☐
4. Recognize definitions in a text ☐
5. Prepare for reading by guessing ideas in a text ☐
6. Recognize and produce a text that presents causes and effects of an event or action ☐
7. Summarize major points in a reading ☐
8. Write a short paragraph answer for an examination ☐

Physiology and Psychology Objectives

1. Explain basic information about sleeping and dreaming ☐
2. Define key terms in physiology and psychology ☐

Reading Assignment 1

WHILE YOU ARE SLEEPING

▽ Getting Ready to Read

EXERCISE 1 Participating in class discussion

Discuss the following questions with your classmates.

1. How much do you sleep? Do you sleep well? Why or why not?
2. Do you know people who sleep a lot or a little? Why do you think they do that?
3. Why do people dream?
4. Do you dream often? Share a recent dream that you can remember.

EXERCISE 2 Reading titles and previewing information

Read the titles of the reading selections listed below. Think about the selections you will read.

Selections

1. "While You Are Sleeping"
2. "What Is Dreaming?"
3. "The ABC's of Dreams"

Discuss the following questions with the members of your study group. Take notes on what your group members know. This will help prepare you to read.

1. Are there *stages*, or steps, of sleep? Explain.

   _____

2. What does your body do while you are sleeping?

   _____

3. What are the reasons for dreaming?

   _____

4. Do dreams have meaning? If so, give two or three examples of dreams and their meanings.

   _____

▽ Focusing on Physiology and Psychology: Key Terms

EXERCISE 3   **Studying key terms**

The readings in this chapter include key terms in the academic fields of physiology *and* psychology. *In Chapter 2, you read about* psychology. *Study the definition of* physiology *below. Then, discuss this question with your classmates: What is the difference between* psychology *and* physiology?

phys • i • ol • o • gy *n.*   the scientific study of the processes, activities, and functions necessary to and characteristic of living things

Here are five other key terms *you will read about in Selections 1 and 2. Put each word in the correct definition sentence. Discuss your answers with your classmates.*

1. *brain waves*	A machine that records the brain's activity is called an _____ .
2. *rapid eye movement (REM) sleep*	_____ are nerve cells that connect parts of the brain.
3. *blood pressure*	The force with which your blood moves through your body is called your _____ . It can be measured by a doctor.
4. *electroencephalogram or EEG*	_____ is the period of sleep in which your eyes move rapidly. It's also called *active sleep.*
5. *neurons*	The brain's electricity activity during sleep is called _____ .

Text Organization

S T R A T E G Y

Process Text Organization

Recognizing the type of organization pattern used in a reading will help you find the most important ideas the writer wants to express. *Process* text organization is commonly used in science and social science texts but may appear in any academic reading that explains a *process*, or series of actions someone does to achieve a particular result. For instance, in Chapter 2, you read about a process: the steps in conducting research by the scientific method.

To identify a process in a text, look for commonly used transitions, or connecting words, that signal *chronological*, or time, order:

Chronological Order Transitions for . . .		
. . . first steps	. . . middle steps	. . . final steps in the process
first	second, third, etc.	last
in the beginning	next	final/finally
to begin	then	in the end
	after that/afterward	
	later	
	meanwhile	

EXERCISE 4   **Preparing to read a process text**

Discuss the following questions with the members of your study group before you read Selection 1.

1. Judging from the title of Selection 1, this reading will tell us the series of actions that occur in what process?
2. Share any other chronological order transitions or other words that might be used to signal time order, and add them to the chart above.

EXERCISE 5   **Annotating steps in the process**

As you read Selection 1, "While You Are Sleeping," look for the steps in the process. Pay attention to words that signal the chronological order of the steps in the process. As you annotate the text, highlight or underline sentences that present steps in the process.

▷ Reading for Information

As you did in Chapters 1 and 2, read Selection 1 the first time nonstop to understand the general ideas. Then, reread it as many times as necessary, marking unfamiliar words and writing definitions of new words next to the text. In particular, look for and mark the key terms. Pay attention to how the terms are used in the reading so that you can understand them better.

Reading Selection 1

WHILE YOU ARE SLEEPING

1   According to ancient stories, people lose control of their minds and nearly die when they sleep. Early researchers thought sleep was a time of mental inactivity.[1] In fact, sleep is an active, complex[2] state.

2   Sleep researchers use an *electroencephalogram*, or *EEG*, to record the brain's electrical activity during sleep. EEG recordings, often called *brain waves*,[3] vary[4] in height and speed as the body's behavior or mental activities change.

3   During a normal night's sleep, brain waves change in height and speed. These EEG changes, along with changes in muscle activity and eye movement, describe six sleep stages. The stages are stage 0, which occurs just before sleep; four stages of quiet sleep; and a stage of rapid eye movement (REM) sleep.

An EEG

1. *inactivity* = a state of not doing anything
2. *complex* = consisting of small parts and therefore difficult to undestand or explain
3. *brain waves* = The form of electrical activity in the brain is described as "waves." Other types of energy we describe in *wave* form are light, sound, and radio.
4. *vary* = to undergo or show change

Stage 0 and Quiet Sleep

4   Imagine that you are participating in a sleep study. You are
hooked up to an EEG and various monitors,[5] and filmed as you
sleep through the night. If you were to watch that film, here's what
you'd see: At first, you are relaxed, with eyes closed, but awake.
This is stage 0. During this stage, your muscles and eye movements
are normal as you fall asleep. The next stages, stages 1 through 4,
are called quiet sleep. In stage 1, your EEG shows slower brain
waves, your breathing deepens,[6] your heartbeat slows, and your
blood pressure drops. Because it contrasts with[7] REM sleep, quiet
sleep is sometimes called non-REM, or NREM, sleep.

5   As you exit stage 1 sleep, your eyes start to roll lazily. The slow
brain waves change to irregular[8] waves similar to those seen in an
awake and mentally active person. Minutes later, stage 2 sleep
begins. Your EEG shows medium speed and strength and some
rapid bursts of brain wave activity. Stage 3 sleep shows brain waves
that are much slower. Next, you are in stage 4 sleep, from which it
is quite difficult to be awakened. If you *were* awakened from this
stage of deep sleep, you would feel sleepy and confused. Your
journey from stage 1 to stage 4 has taken about twenty minutes.

REM Sleep

6   After thirty to forty minutes in stage 4, you quickly return to
stage 2 sleep and then begin a special stage in which your eyes
move rapidly under your closed eyelids. This is called REM sleep, or
active sleep. As in stage 1, your EEG resembles that of an awake,
alert person, but now your physiological[9] activities—heartbeat,
breathing, blood pressure—also look the same as when you are
awake. Strangely, although EEG and other measures resemble those
of an awake person, your muscles show almost no movement.
Sudden quick movements appear, especially in your face and
hands, as neurons[10] cause your arms and legs to move. Most dreams
occur during REM sleep.

5. *monitors* = pieces of equipment that look like televisions and show information
   or pictures
6. *deepens* = becomes deeper
7. *contrasts with* = is different or opposite from
8. *irregular* = not regular
9. *physiological* = relating to the scientific study of the processes, activities, and
   functions necessary to and characteristic of living things
10. *neurons* = nerve cells

A Night's Sleep

7   Most people pass through the cycle[11] of sleep stages four to six times each night. Each cycle lasts about ninety minutes, but with a changing pattern of stages and stage duration.[12] Early in the night, most of the time is spent in stages 3 and 4, with only a few minutes in REM. As sleep continues, though, it is dominated by[13] stage 2 and REM, from which sleepers finally awaken.

8   The night's sleep that was just described is the ideal, but things don't always run so smoothly. If you're like most people, you've probably had nights of tossing and turning, difficulty falling asleep, or some other sleep-related problems. This makes sense when you consider that sleeping is a complex process.

From *Essentials of Psychology*, by D. A. Bernstein & P. W. Nash. Copyright © 2001 Houghton Mifflin Company. Reprinted with permission.

◹ Assessing Your Learning

Recognizing Words that Signal Process

EXERCISE 6   **Annotating steps in the process**

Compare your annotations of Selection 1, "While You Are Sleeping," with those of your classmates. Then discuss the following questions with the members of your study group.

1. What process is explained in Selection 1?
2. How many steps are in the process?
3. Does the process occur only once, or do the steps repeat themselves?
4. Is the process easy or difficult to follow? Explain.
5. What chronological order transitions are used to show the time order of steps in the process? Do any other words help you follow the steps of the process? If so, which words?

11. *cycle* = a series of related events that happen again and again in the same order
12. *duration* = the length of time that something continues
13. *dominated by* = under the power and control of someone or something

▷ Demonstrating Comprehension

EXERCISE 7 Checking for chronological order in process texts

The seven sentences below present the steps in the process described in the first section of Selection 1. Check your comprehension of this section by putting the sentences into the correct chronological order. Do this <u>without</u> looking back at the text. Then, use your annotations and the reading itself to check the order of the process.

1. _____ Your brain waves slow down.

2. _____ You are sleeping deeply.

3. _____ You experience rapid bursts of brain wave activity.

4. _____ You return to stage 2 sleep and begin rapid eye movement sleep.

5. _____ Your eyes start to roll and your brain waves are not regular.

6. _____ Your eyes are closed, but you're still awake.

7. _____ Your heartbeat and blood pressure slows.

For each sentence above, mark the paragraph in Selection 1 that contains the idea. Share your answers with your classmates.

EXERCISE 8 Using chronological order transitions

Next, write a paragraph using the seven sentences from Exercise 7. Begin your paragraph by adding a topic sentence (main idea sentence) that introduces the process being explained. Add chronological order transitions such as those in the box before Selection 1, or use any other words that will clarify the time order of the process. Share your paragraph with one of your classmates.

Example Topic Sentences for a Process Paragraph

Psychologists use several steps in order to hypnotize patients.

If you have trouble sleeping, here are a few steps that may help you.

These example topic sentences do not match the topic of Selection 1, but they are good examples of topic sentences for a process paragraph.

EXERCISE **9**   **Finding the main idea**

Read the three sentences below. Put a check mark next to the sentence that best expresses the overall main idea of Selection 1, "While You Are Sleeping."

A. ———— Researchers don't really know what occurs during sleep.

B. ———— Sleep is an active, complex state.

C. ———— Two types of sleep are quiet sleep and active sleep.

D. ———— The reading is about sleep.

Next, match each of the sentences above that you did <u>not</u> choose with one of the following descriptions. Put the letter of the sentence next to the appropriate description. Share your answers with classmates.

———— This sentence is too general. It only tells what the reading is about.

———— This sentence is too specific. It tells about only one idea in the reading.

———— This sentence could be a main idea sentence, but it's untrue, according to the reading.

STRATEGY

Recognizing Details in Reading

The main idea of Selection 1 is stated above. The major points in this reading include sentences that introduce each stage of sleep. In addition, the selection contains many *details*, or specific pieces of information, about the sleep stages. As with other types of supporting sentences, detail sentences commonly appear <u>after</u> major point sentences. However, detail sentences may also appear <u>before</u> *general* concluding sentences in paragraphs.

To identify details, look for words containing specific information, such as *descriptions* and *facts*. Read this passage from "The Wild Boy of Aveyron" (in Chapter 2). Again, note how the major point sentences contain more *general* ideas, whereas the detail sentences contain more *specific* information.

General Idea

In Paris, <u>scientists expected to observe</u> what philosopher

General Idea

Jean-Jacques Rousseau had called the "<u>noble savage</u>." After all, here

General Idea

was a <u>human being who had grown up untouched</u> by the evils of

Description

society. But what scientists found instead was a <u>frightened creature</u>

Fact   Fact   Fact

who <u>moved like a wild animal</u> and <u>ate garbage</u>. He <u>spent most</u>

Facts

<u>of his time</u> <u>silently rocking</u> but would <u>snarl</u> and <u>attack anyone</u>

who <u>tried to touch him</u>.

Major Point Sentences { ... }

Detail Sentences { ... }

EXERCISE 10 **Identifying major points and details**

Read the paragraph below, taken from Selection 1. Mark each sentence as either MP, a major point, or D, a detail sentence. Think about which sentences contain general ideas and which contain specific information. Discuss your answers with the rest of your class.

Imagine that you are participating in a sleep study. You are hooked up to an EEG and various monitors, and filmed as you sleep through the night. If you were to watch that film, here's what you'd see: At first, you are relaxed, with eyes closed, but awake. This is stage 0. During this stage, your muscles and eye movements are normal as you fall asleep. The next stages, stages 1 through 4, are called quiet sleep. In stage 1, your EEG shows slower brain waves, your breathing deepens, your heartbeat slows, and your blood pressure drops. Because it contrasts with REM sleep, quiet sleep is sometimes called non-REM, or NREM, sleep.

EXERCISE **11**   Scanning for details

Each sentence below has one detail that is not correct. Scan Selection 1 to find each detail, and correct the detail sentence to make it accurate. Compare your answers with your classmates'.

1. During an irregular night's sleep, brain waves change in height and speed.

2. Stages 1 through 3 are called quiet sleep.

3. Your journey from stage 1 to stage 4 has taken about ten minutes.

4. Most dreams occur during non-REM sleep.

5. Most people pass through the cycle of sleep stages one to six times each night.

6. Each cycle lasts about ninety minutes, but with the same pattern of stages and stage duration.

POWER GRAMMAR

Recognizing Definitions in a Text

Academic readings often provide definitions of important ideas or words in the text. Each definition may be a one-word synonym, a word with a similar meaning or the same meaning as another word, or a synonymous phrase. Pay attention to certain markers—punctuation and or words that may signal definitions. Another way to recognize a definition is a key idea or word that may appear in *italic* or **bold** type.

Four common definition markers

► Commas

A definition may be marked by a comma or commas following a key idea or word. If the definition appears in the middle of a sentence, it will be set off with two commas. If the definition comes at the end of a sentence, it will begin with a comma and end with a period. A definition after a keyword is called an *appositive*.

Example

Keyword   Definition

(Daydreaming,) the act of seeing images or having unfocused

thoughts that are different from a person's reality, can make a

person feel calm in a stressful situation.

▶ Long dashes (—)

After the key idea or word, a definition may be set off with one or two long dashes. In the middle of a sentence, two dashes will be used. At the end of the sentence, one dash separates the key word and its definition. The definition may also appear first, and the key idea or word within the dashes.

Example

Definition   Keyword

The body's natural cycles—called (circadian rhythms) —occur

in a roughly 25-hour period.

▶ *Or/That is*

An important idea or word may be followed by a comma or commas and the term *or* or *that is* to introduce a definition. A comma appears before *or*, and commas separate *that is*.

Example

Keyword   Definition

(Insomnia,) or the inability to sleep, is sometimes caused by stress.

▶ Parentheses ( )

A keyword or idea may be followed by a set of parentheses containing a definition.

Example

Keyword   Definition

(Jet lag) (a tired and confused feeling resulting from high-speed

air travel through several time zones) commonly occurs when

you fly across the country.

EXERCISE 12   **Identifying definitions in a text**

Circle the keyword(s) or idea(s) and underline the definition(s) in each sentence below. Compare your answers with a partner's.

1. Sleep researchers use an *electroencephalogram*, or *EEG*, to record the brain's electrical activity during sleep.
2. EEG recordings, often called *brain waves*, vary in height and speed as the body's behavior or mental activities change.
3. Stage 0, which occurs just before sleep; four stages of quiet sleep; and rapid eye movement (REM) sleep.
4. Because it contrasts with REM sleep, quiet sleep is sometimes called non-REM, or NREM, sleep.
5. After thirty to forty minutes in stage 4, you quickly return to stage 2 sleep and then begin a special stage in which your eyes move rapidly under your closed eyelids. This is called REM sleep, or *active sleep*.

▷ Questions for Discussion

Focusing on Psychology and Physiology

Discuss the following questions in small groups.

1. Reread the steps in the sleep process. Can you confirm any of the stages by your own sleep habits or those of someone you know? Explain.
2. Do you have any problems with sleeping? If so, explain.
3. Have you or someone you know ever been awakened suddenly from sleep? If so, how did you or that person act? From the information in Selection 1, what stage of sleep do you think you or the other person was in?

▷ Learning Vocabulary

EXERCISE 13   **Identifying word families and parts of speech**

As you learned in Chapter 2, words belong to families containing similar words with different endings. The words on the next page appear in Selection 1. Next to each word, identify its part of speech (n., v., adj., adv.).

Word family "members"	Part of speech	Sentence
active		
activity		
relaxed*		
relaxation		
difficult		
difficulty		
lose		
loss		
continual		
continue		
rapid		
rapidly		
sleepy		
sleepers		
complex		
complexity		
research		
researcher		
mental		
mentality		

Relaxed can be a verb or an adjective. Pay attention to how this word is used in the sentence(s) in Selection 1.

Next, find a sentence from Selection 1 in which the words in the chart appear. Write the sentence next to the part of speech. Underline the word from the list in the sentence. For each listed word that does not appear in the reading, write your own sentence using the word. Share your sentences with another classmate.

Example:

active ___adj___ The brain is active in all sleep stages.

EXERCISE 14 **Using the correct part of speech**

Complete the following paragraph with the correct parts of speech. Circle one of each pair of underlined words. The first has been done for you as an example.

INSOMNIA

Insomnia is the most common sleep-related problem, and it is a

(**1**) difficult / difficulty one to solve. *Insomnia* means not being

able to (**2**) sleep / sleepy. If people (**3**) lose / loss sleep, they feel

tired during the day. Some (**4**) researchers / research believe that if

people are depressed, they may be more likely to have insomnia.

However, depression is not the only cause of insomnia. A

psychology textbook says that people with (**5**) mentality / mental

problems have more insomnia. What is the solution for this

(**6**) complex / complexity problem? Some doctors recommend

sleeping pills. Others suggest that (**7**) relaxation / relaxed will help.

An (**8**) activity / active lifestyle may also help get rid of insomnia. If

insomniacs do physical (**9**) activity / active, their bodies will feel

exhausted and they may fall asleep more (**10**) rapidly / rapid.

Insomnia (**11**) continual / continues to be a serious problem.

EXERCISE 15   Reviewing academic vocabulary

Complete the sentences below by using the academic vocabulary words from the list below. Use each word only once. The first one is done for you.

researchers	complex	vary	mental
cycle	occur	duration	normal

(1) _Researchers_ have studied people's sleeping habits. They have

discovered that sleeping is a (2) _____ process made up of six

stages. During each stage of sleep, many changes (3) _____ in the

body. Scientists have found that in a (4) _____ night's sleep, a

person usually repeats the (5) _____ of stages over and over. Of

course, sleeping habits (6) _____ from person to person. The (7)

_____ of one's night of sleep depends on many factors, such as

physical activity and (8) _____ health.

EXERCISE 16   Reviewing academic vocabulary

Put a check mark next to any of these academic vocabulary words from Selection 1 that you already know.

abandon(ed)	eventually	philosopher	specifically
psychologist(s)	contact(s)	environment(s)	
interact	highlight	normal	

Add unfamiliar words to your academic vocabulary list. For each unfamiliar word, write the word and its definition, and write a sentence using the word.

Reading Assignment 2

▷ Reading for a Purpose

STRATEGY

Predicting Content before Reading

Predicting the content of a reading beforehand helps you prepare yourself for reading. If you try to guess about the ideas in a reading before you read, you will focus on whether your ideas were correct or not.

Here are a few methods for predicting content:

► Preview the title, art, and any headings in a reading. Write down or think about what you already know about this topic before reading.

► Ask questions before reading. Use information from the title, art, and headings to write questions about the content. Then, when you read, you can look for the answers.

► Take a short test on the topic of the reading before you read. This will help you find out how much you already know about a topic, and it will help you focus your reading. When you read, you'll be checking your prereading ideas about the content.

EXERCISE 17 Predicting content before reading

Test your knowledge of dreaming. Mark the following statements T for True or F for False. Compare your answers with those of other members of your study group.

1. _____ Dreams rarely last longer than a few minutes.

2. _____ Dreams often follow logical patterns.

3. _____ A person's daytime activities probably have a great impact on her or his dreams.

4. _____ Blind people dream.

5. _____ Nonhuman animals like cats probably dream.

6. _____ According to Sigmund Freud, dreams reflect our hidden desires.

7. _____ Dreams may be just meaningless responses to a person's body activities during REM sleep.

8. _____ Research gives us strong evidence that people use dreams to solve their daily problems.

STRATEGY

Recognizing Words that Signal Cause and Effect

Cause-and-*effect* organization is another common organizational pattern used in academic readings. For example, a history text may explain the *causes* of a war, or an economics textbook may present the *effects* of a worldwide economic depression. A physiology reading might explain the *causes* and *effects* of a disease, whereas a psychology text may present the *causes* and *effects* of a mental disorder.

Text Organization

Here are some common features that signal cause-effect organization:

► Cause-effect texts generally follow these sequences:

Example:

Cause ⟶ Effect

<u>Depression</u> may also cause <u>insomnia</u>.

Example:

Effect ⟶ Cause

One reason why <u>people</u> may <u>have insomnia</u> is <u>that they lead inactive lives.</u>

A text may emphasize either the *cause(s)* or the *effect(s)* of the situation, problem, event, and so on, or present both the cause(s) and effect(s) of something.

► Certain words are commonly present in cause-effect sentences:

why	reason	impact	produce	as a result
because	source	result	result in	consequently
since	root	outcome	generate	therefore
cause	leads to			

▷ Reading for Information

As you did with Selection 1, read Selection 2 to find information, especially causes and effects.

► *Read the text once without a dictionary.*
► *Then, read it as many times as necessary.*
► *Mark important ideas with a highlighter pen or by underlining, and write words in the margins about these ideas.*
► *Annotate sentences that present causes or effects.*

Reading Selection 2

WHAT IS DREAMING?

1   The brain is active in all sleep stages. However, dreams differ from other mental activity in sleep because they are usually story-like. They may be as short as a few seconds or last for many minutes. Dreams may be organized or chaotic,[1] realistic or fantastic,[2] boring or exciting. Sometimes, dreams lead to creative solutions or ideas about waking problems. For example, after trying for days to write a story about good and evil in the same person, author Robert Louis Stevenson[3] supposedly dreamed about a man who drank a magic drink that turned him into a monster. This dream may have inspired[4] *The Strange Case of Dr. Jekyll and Mr. Hyde.*

1. *chaotic* = disorganized and confusing
2. *fantastic* = strange or unreal
3. *Robert Louis Stevenson* = British writer of essays, poetry, and novels, including a story of a doctor who changed his personality when he drank a special drink
4. *inspired* = to stimulate somebody to creativity or action

2   Although they may seem strange, dreams often contain a certain amount of logic.[5] For example, when parts of dream reports were reordered, readers could correctly say which had been rearranged and which were left the same. A second study showed that dream reports commonly described one person changing into another or one object turning into another object. However, transformation[6] of objects into people or vice versa[7] are rare.

3   Daytime activities may have some influence on dream content, though their impact is probably minor.[8] In one study, people wore red-colored glasses for a few minutes just before going to sleep. Although they did not know the purpose of the study, the next morning they reported more red images in their dreams than people who had not worn the glasses. It is also sometimes possible to direct dream content. This is especially true during lucid[9] dreaming in which the sleeper is aware of dreaming *while a dream is happening.*

4   Research leaves little doubt that everyone dreams during every night of normal sleep. Even blind people dream, although their experiences are usually not visual. Whether you remember a dream depends on how you sleep and wake up. Recall is better if you awaken suddenly and lie quietly while writing or tape-recording what you remember.

5   Why do we dream? There are many theories.[10] Some see dreaming as a basic process that lets us analyze[11] and put together information. Research suggests that even nonhuman animals dream. After researchers disabled the neurons that cause REM sleep paralysis,[12] sleeping cats ran around and attacked unseen objects, probably from their dreams.

5. *logic* = a set of sensible and correct reasons
6. *transformation* = a complete change in the appearance or character of someone or something
7. *vice versa* = with the order or meaning of something reversed
8. *minor* = of little importance
9. *lucid* = having full use of one's mental powers
10. *theory* = a set of statements or principles, based on limited information or knowledge, that is designed to explain an event or a group of events and that can be used to make predictions about natural phenomena
11. *analyze* = to examine something in detail
12. *paralysis* = partial or complete loss of the ability to move or feel sensations in a part of the body

6   According to Sigmund Freud,[13] dreams are a form of *wish fulfillment*.[14] They are a way to satisfy unconscious desires or solve unconscious problems that are too upsetting to deal with consciously.[15] Thus, sexual desires might appear in a dream as the motions of a horseback ride. Conflicting feelings about a parent might appear as a dream about a fight. Seeing patients' dreams as a "road to knowledge of the unconscious," Freud used their meaning as part of his treatment of psychological problems.

7   In contrast, the *activation-synthesis* theory sees dreams as the meaningless, random[16] effects of REM sleep. According to this theory, the back part of the brain creates messages that *activate*[17] the brain. Dreams result as the brain connects, or *synthesizes*, these messages as best as it can, using stored memories and current feelings to translate random brain activity into something more logical. From this viewpoint, dreams represent the brain's attempt to make sense of meaningless stimulation[18] during sleep, in much the same way that we try to find meaningful shapes in clouds while awake.

8   Even if dreams come from random brain activity, their content may still have psychological importance. According to the *problem-solving theory*, dreams give people a chance to review and deal with problems they face during waking hours. One study investigated the dreams of divorcing or recently divorced women. Those who were depressed dreamed mostly of the past. Nondepressed women more often had problem-solving dreams as well as dreams covering the past, present, and future. Although there is no strong research support for problem-solving theory, the mental style or current concerns of the dreamer *can* affect the ways in which dreams are organized and remembered.

From *Essentials of Psychology*, by D. A. Bernstein & P. W. Nash. Copyright © 2001 Houghton Mifflin Company. Reprinted with permission.

---

13. *Freud* = an Austrian psychologist of the late 1800s who studied how the mind words and who believed that early experiences were important for understanding behavior and; is known as the founder of psychoanalysis
14. *wish fulfillment* = in psychoanalytic theory, the satisfaction of a desire, need, or impulse through a dream
15. *consciously* = with wakeful awareness
16. *random* = without any definite plan, purpose, or pattern
17. *activate* = to make something start working
18. *stimulation* = the act of causing activity or increased action in somebody or something

▷ Assessing Your Learning

Demonstrating Comprehension

EXERCISE 18 Identifying major points

With a partner, put a check mark next to the sentence in the chart that best expresses the major points of each paragraph in Selection 2, "What Is Dreaming?" Check your answers by looking back at the reading and your annotation.

Paragraph	Major points
1	_____ A dream is a story-like activity in your mind that has many different forms. _____ The brain is active all the time that you sleep.
2	_____ Dreams may seem strange to us. _____ The activity in dreams follows logical rules.
3	_____ People can sometimes control the content of their dreams. _____ What happens to us during the day can affect our dreams.
4	_____ Everyone dreams in a normal night's sleep. _____ People remember their dreams better if they write them down.
5	_____ Nonhuman animals like cats dream. _____ Several theories explain dreaming, including one idea that dreaming may be a basic analytical process.
6	_____ Freud had a theory about why people dream. _____ According to Freud, people dream to solve their problems or fulfill their desires.
7	_____ Dreams may simply be a meaningless brain activity. _____ The brain connects messages by using memories and feelings.
8	_____ The mental condition of the dreamer can affect her or his dreams. _____ Dreams may help people fix daytime problems.

EXERCISE 19   **Checking your self-test**

Check the answers to the True/False questions you answered in Exercise 17 before reading. Next to each statement, write the paragraph number in which the idea is stated. Rewrite false statements to make them true. Compare your answers with those of the other members of your study group.

EXERCISE 20   **Constructing a main idea sentence**

Selection 2 does not have a clearly stated main idea sentence. Work with a partner to construct a general *main idea sentence that encompasses, or includes, all the major points. Remember that the main idea sentence should include the* topic *plus the writer's attitude, opinion, or idea* about *it. Share your sentence with your classmates.*

Text Organization

EXERCISE 21   **Studying cause-effect organization**

Answer the following items. Write your answers on separate paper.

1. Selection 2 presents *causes*, or reasons, for _____ .
2. List the four *causes* you find in the reading.
3. With your partner, write a short paragraph to briefly explain the four causes presented in the reading. You do not need to include all the details about each cause in the reading. Include at least one sentence about each cause. On separate paper, begin your paragraph with sentences like the ones below:

   The reading tells us four causes, or reasons, for _____ .

   One theory is that . . .

▷ Questions for Discussion

EXERCISE 22   **Transferring ideas to personal experience**

Share your cause paragraphs with the members of your study group. Then, discuss the following questions.

1. Consider your own dreams. Which of the four causes presented in the reading makes the most sense to you? Explain.

2. Have you had dreams that support any of the four theories presented in the reading? If so, briefly tell about your dream and why it supports the theory or theories about dreams.
3. Do you usually remember your dreams? If so, for how long?
4. Do you have recurring dreams? If so, what are they about?

▷ Reading Journal

Write a reading journal entry on one of the following topics:

1. Write about your sleep habits. Do you sleep well? How long do you usually sleep? Do you have any problems sleeping? What do you think are the reasons for your sleeping problems? What do you do when you cannot sleep?
2. Write the story of one memorable dream you have had.

▷ Learning Vocabulary

POWER GRAMMAR

Working with Word Families

Paying attention to the endings, or forms, of each "member," or part of speech, in a word family will help you use the correct form. Six common adjective endings are underlined in the words below:

-al	logical	Dreams are usually logical.
-ive	active	The brain is active during sleep.
-ing	boring	Dreams may be boring.
-ful	meaningful	They can also be meaningful.
-less	meaningless	One dream theory describes dreams as meaningless brain activities.
-ous	conscious	Sometimes people are conscious while they are dreaming.
-able, -ible	possible	It is sometimes possible to direct dream content.

EXERCISE 23   **Studying adjective endings**

Complete the words in the text below with the correct adjective endings.
Use a dictionary to help you, if necessary. Compare your answers with
a partner's. The first one is done for you.

Hypnosis

Hypnosis is an interest_ing_ (**1**) technique that is sometimes used as

psychologic_____ (**2**) treatment. It started in the 1700s, when an Austrian

doctor, Frank Mesmer, became fam_____ (**3**) for his ability to treat

vari_____ (**4**) physical problems with "mesmerism." Mesmer's technique

was an early form of hypnosis.

The word *hypnosis* comes from the Greek word *hypnos*, meaning

"sleep." However, hypnotized people are not sleeping. Their minds are

act_____ (**5**) and awake. Hypnosis is a condition that is caused by special

techniques. Usually, hypnosis begins with suggestions that the person feels

peace_____ (**6**) and sleepy. The hypnotist then focuses the person's

attention on a set of motions, like a swing_____ (**7**) watch or necklace.

When a person is hypnotized, he or she is not consci_____ (**8**) of his or

her actions.

The hypnotist controls what the person does. For this reason, some

people believe hypnosis is a danger_____ (**9**) activity. Doctors can use

hypnosis to help their patients but must be care_____ (**10**) about how they

use this type of treatment.

EXERCISE 24   **Reviewing academic vocabulary**

Use each of the academic vocabulary words on the left to complete a
sentence on the right. Check your answer with a partner. Use a dictionary,
if necessary.

1. ____ creative, *adj.*

2. ____ minor, *adj.*

3. ____ investigated, *v.*

4. ____ logical, *adj.*

5. ____ stimulation, *n.*

6. ____ random, *adj.*

7. ____ conflict, *n.*

8. ____ aware, *adj.*

9. ____ transformation, *n.*

10. ____ analyze, *v.*

A. Events in dreams usually follow a _____ order.

B. Some people believe that dreams may simply happen because of the brain's _____ by other parts of the body.

C. Are you _____ that you are dreaming when you dream?

D. _____ of objects into people is rare in dreams.

E. Daily activities may have only a _____ impact on dreams.

F. Dreams may help us _____ and put together information.

G. If your parents have a _____, you may dream about a fight.

H. Dreams may show meaningless, _____ activities that have no plan or purpose.

I. Researchers have _____ the reasons why we dream.

J. Dreams may help us find _____ solutions to problems.

EXERCISE `25` **Reviewing academic vocabulary**

Put a check mark next to the academic vocabulary words from Selection 1 that you already know.

affect	analyze	author	aware
conflict	contrast	create/creative	depressed
image(s)	impact	investigate(d)	logic/logical
mental	minor	normal	process
psychological	random	research/researcher(s)	sexual
stimulation	style	tape	theory(ies)
transformation	visual		

Add unfamiliar words to your academic vocabulary list. For each unfamiliar word, write the word and its definition, and write a sentence using the word.

Reading Assignment 3

THE ABC'S OF DREAMS

▷ Reading for a Purpose

EXERCISE 26 **Predicting content before reading**

Selection 3 is titled "The ABC's of Dreams." Find out how much you know about this topic by taking the following self-test. Circle the letter that represents the best answer. Compare your answers with those of the rest of your class.

1. Choose the sentence that best describes scientists' general opinion about dreams.

   A. Dreams are a biological (related to the body) process.
   B. Dreams are a psychological process.
   C. Dreams are a process of both the body and the mind.
   D. Scientists don't know if dreams are biological or psychological.

2. Dreams may occur because of

   A. our body's random brain activities.
   B. recent problems in our lives.
   C. both of the above.

3. One meaning of dreams about airplanes may be that

   A. you want to take a trip.
   B. you want to be a pilot.
   C. you are afraid of taking a trip.

4. One analysis of dreams about babies says that the meaning of these dreams depends on

   A. what the baby looks like.
   B. what the baby is doing.
   C. both of the above.

5. According to one dream analyst, which of the following sentences best describes one dream that includes a chase?

   A. You want to solve a problem, so someone is chasing you.
   B. You are worried about a problem, so in the dream, you chase someone else.
   C. You are trying to escape your problem, so someone is chasing you.

▷ Reading for Information

As you did with Selection 2, read Selection 3 once without a dictionary. Then, read it as many times as necessary. Mark important ideas with a highlighter pen or by underlining, and write words in the margins about these ideas. Underline and define unfamiliar words.

A Drawing of a Dream

Reading Selection 3

THE ABC'S OF DREAMS

1   Given that[1] scientists are not even in agreement about whether dreams are psychological or biological, there are no reliable methods for interpreting dreams. Dreams may be random, they may be involved in putting together information or in solving problems at the subconscious level, they may arise from the unconscious, or they may be responses to neural activity.

---

1. *Given that . . .* = knowing that . . .

2   Sometimes people feel that they understand the meaning behind a dream. Others worry about what a recurring dream may mean. But even if we are merely creating stories around random neural firings, it is likely that recent events or problems in our lives would be the most accessible in the production of those stories. Even when a reasonable interpretation is given for a dream, how would we be certain that it is correct?

3   Scientists today may not think that we can interpret our dreams, but many non-scientists do. Hundreds of books attempt to explain the meaning of dreams, and in different cultures, those interpretations vary. You can find many sources of information about dreams and their meaning in books, magazines, or articles on the Internet. Here are some examples of dream interpretations, starting with the "ABC's":

Aging

4   Dreaming about old people, or your own aging may have several different meanings. According to some people, an old man may symbolize wisdom and forgiveness, and an old woman—life and death. In general, some people believe aging may represent wisdom that a person acquires through experience. This dream may also be a reflection of your concerns about aging. If you are thinking about your mortality[2] and do not welcome maturing and age, some say that the dream may be bringing out some of your worries.

Airplane

5   If you are a passenger in a plane you may be subconsciously thinking about someone or something that is far away and you wish to get in touch, according to some dream analysts. If you are the pilot it suggest that you have a sense of control and an underlying confidence that you will succeed in your endeavors.[3]

Baby

6   The meaning of this dream depends on what the baby looked like and was doing. Generally, many people say that babies represent innocence, great potential and new beginnings. According to some people, the baby is the purest form of a human being and its possibilities are endless. They believe that all the potential good of the entire universe can usually be seen and felt in a new born baby. Superstition based interpretations suggest that if the baby in your

2. *mortality* = the condition of being human and having to die
3. *endeavors* = attempts or efforts to do something new or different

dream is beautiful you may experience new happiness and feelings of security. An ugly baby suggests that you may not be trusting your friends and that you may be concerned about their motives;[4] sick babies indicate that you may have some very difficult times in your immediate future, according to some dream experts.

Blood

7   It is the life giving, vital part of our physiology, and, people believe it may symbolize our strengths and weaknesses, our physical and mental health. If you are currently experiencing a very difficult time in your life, you may have dreams with bloody and frightening images. Don't worry, dream analysts say; you may be venting[5] your fears! Some believe that when you see blood in your dream, the distressing[6] situation in your life, which is at the root of the dream, has come to an end and the worst is over.

Car

8   The car in your dream can symbolize the larger self or the physical self, according to some dream experts. They suggest that you consider all of the details in the dream, including the emotional aspects of it. Is the road difficult, going up hill or down hill, and who is in the driver's seat? Some people believe that recurring car dreams usually deal with issues of control.

Chase

9   Folklore interpretations say that if you are looking at a chase or participating in it, you will have a comfortable old age. Although this may be comforting, there is a more realistic understanding of this activity in a dream. Others say that if you are being chased, maybe you are running away or trying to escape those things that are frightening and unpleasant. It may be your own habits and negative behaviors. If you are doing the chasing, it may be that you are expressing some aggressive[7] feelings toward others, or you are pursuing[8] a very difficult goal, according to some dream analysts.

Source of paragraphs 1 and 2: *Introduction to Psychology*, 2001.
Evanston, IL: McDougal-Littell, p. 90. Source of dream interpretations:
http://wiccachile.tripod.com/moon/dream1.htm.

4. *motives* = emotions or needs that cause a person to act in a certain way
5. *venting* = forcefully expressing your feelings
6. *distressing* = worrisome or upsetting
7. *aggressive* = showing hostile behavior

Master Student Tip

Writing a summary, or brief report of major ideas in a reading, is a useful academic skill. Many academic assignments require summarizing.

Here are some quick guidelines for writing a summary.

▶ First, you need to **fully understand the text** you are going to summarize. Discuss a text with classmates. Ask questions of your instructor.

▶ Next, include only the most important ideas in a text, not the details.

▶ **Identify and mark** the **main idea and major points** in the text.

▶ **Begin with a main idea sentence that states the title and author (if known) and main idea of the text.**

▽ Assessing Your Learning

Demonstrating Comprehension

EXERCISE 27 Expressing the main idea

Write one sentence to express the main idea of Selection 3. Compare your sentence with a partner's. Then, share your best ideas and rewrite your sentence, if appropriate. Share your sentence with the rest of your class.

EXERCISE 28 Checking your self-test

Check the answers to the self-test you took in Exercise 26 before reading. Next to each question, write the paragraph number in which the idea is stated.

EXERCISE 29 Checking comprehension

Read the following statements. Work with your partner to mark each statement True (T) or False (F) based on information from Selection 3. Rewrite false statements to make them true. Check your answers by looking back at the reading. Share your answers with the rest of your class.

1. _____ Scientists believe there are several dependable ways to analyze the meaning of dreams.

2. _____ Many nonscientists have written about the subject of dream interpretation.

3. _____ One idea is that dreams about aging may show that people are worried about getting old.

4. _____ In general, babies symbolize new beginnings in dreams.

5. _____ The reading says that if you are having many problems and you dream about blood, you should be concerned.

6. _____ The meaning of dreams about cars depends on the direction the car is going and who is driving, according to the reading.

EXERCISE 30 Evaluating summaries

Work with a partner to evaluate the three summaries printed below. First, quickly reread Selection 1, "While You Are Sleeping." Then, read each summary below, and decide which is the most effective summary. Discuss the reasons for your choice with the rest of your class.

Summary A

The reading "What Is Dreaming?" from a book by Douglas A. Bernstein and Peggy W. Nash explains that the brain is active in all sleep stages. However, dreams differ from other mental activity in sleep because they are usually story-like. Dreams may seem strange, but they often contain a certain amount of logic. Daytime activities may influence dream content. Also, research leaves little doubt that everyone dreams. There are many theories about why we dream. Some see dreaming as a basic process. According to Sigmund Freud, dreams are a form of *wish fulfillment*. The *activation-synthesis* theory sees dreams as meaningless. According to the *problem-solving theory*, dreams give people a chance to review and deal with problems.

Summary B

"What Is Dreaming?" is an interesting article that explains all about dreams. It says that dreams may be short or long, exciting or boring. This is true, based on my own dreams. The article also says that people sometimes remember that they are dreaming *while* the dream is taking place. This has happened to me before. I was surprised to learn that blind people and even cats dream. That's fantastic. I read four theories about why we dream. The one that I agree with is the *problem-solving theory*. I think that people dream to solve their daily problems. I learned a lot from this article and I enjoyed reading it very much.

Summary C

The reading "What Is Dreaming?" from a book by Douglas R. Bernstein and Peggy W. Nash describes dreaming and theories about why people dream. Dreams are story-like and logical, the article says. Researchers are not certain if dreams are influenced by a person's daytime experiences, but they conclude that everyone dreams in a normal night of sleep. The article also explains four theories related to dreaming. One theory is that dreams help people analyze information. The theory of Sigmund Freud says that dreams reflect a person's desires. Another theory suggests that dreams have no important meaning. According to the reading, a fourth theory says that dreams help people solve problems.

EXERCISE 31 **Writing a summary**

Write a summary of Selection 3, "The ABC's of Dreaming." Begin with a main idea sentence. Then, use the headings in the readings to determine the major points of the reading. After you write your summary, work with your study group to evaluate each other's summaries. Share ideas from each other's summaries to revise your summary.

▽ Questions for Discussion

EXERCISE 32 **Linking ideas to personal experience**

Discuss the following questions with in your study group. Then, write answers to your questions on separate paper. Write in complete sentences.

1. Think about your own dreams. In general, do you think you understand your dreams, as the reading suggests?
2. What is your opinion of the example dream interpretations in the reading? In general, do you think the writer's ideas about the meanings of *aging, airplanes, babies, blood, cars,* and *chases* in dreams make sense? Why or why not?
3. Do you know any superstitions about the meaning of dreams? For example, what do you think *water* represents in a dream? Where do you get your ideas from? Do any of the ideas come from superstitions in your home country? If so, explain some of them.

▽ Reading Journal

The famous inventor and artist Leonardo da Vinci wrote: "The eye sees a thing more clearly in dreams than the imagination when awake." Do you agree or disagree with this statement? Write a one-page journal entry about whether a person sees things clearly when he or she dreams. Use examples of your dreams to support your ideas. Also, include at least one idea from Selection 3, "The ABC's of Dreams."

▷ Learning Vocabulary

EXERCISE 33 **Working with adjectives**

Earlier, you studied the following underlined adjective endings:

-al	men<u>tal</u>	-ing	interest<u>ing</u>
-ive	ac<u>tive</u>	-ful	care<u>ful</u>
-less	care<u>less</u>	-ous	vari<u>ous</u>
-able, -ible	depend<u>able</u>		

Use the correct adjective endings to complete the words in the sentences below. Do not use a dictionary. Do not look back at the reading. After you finish, check your answers by looking back at Selection 3, in which the words appear. The first one is done for you.

1. Given that scientists are not even in agreement about whether

dreams are psychologic _al_ or biologic_____, there are no reli_____

methods for interpreting dreams. Dreams may be random, they may

be involved in putting together information or in solving problems at

the subconsc_____ level, they may arise from the unconsc_____, or

they may be responses to neur_____ activity.

2. It is the life giv_____, vit_____ part of our physiology and it may

symbolize our strengths and weaknesses, our physic_____ and

ment _____ health. If you are currently experiencing a very difficult

time in your life, you may have dreams with bloody and frighten_____

images.

3. Consider all of the details in the dream, including the emotion_____

aspects of it.

4. If you are doing the chasing, it may be that you are expressing some

aggress_____ feelings towards others or you are pursuing a very

difficult goal.

Master Student Tip

▼ **Short-Answer Examinations**

Many professors include short-answer questions on their tests.

To answer short-answer questions well on examinations, follow these two basic steps:

1. First, read the question carefully and make sure you understand what information to include in the answer.

2. Pay close attention to the *directive* words in the question. Words like *explain, contrast,* and *describe* indicate the way the answer should be presented.

3. Be sure to answer all the question(s) completely with your written answer. Answers generally range from several sentences to essay-length.

EXERCISE 34 **Reviewing academic vocabulary**

Match the academic words on the left with the definitions on the right.

1. _____ reliable

2. _____ response

3. _____ pursue

4. _____ symbolize

5. _____ aspects

6. _____ indicate

7. _____ interpret

8. _____ vital

A. parts or features of a situation, idea, problem, etc.

B. to represent or identify something by a symbol

C. to explain the meaning of something

D. to show the way to or the direction of

E. extremely important or necessary

F. a reply or an answer

G. to try to get or accomplish something

H. dependable

EXERCISE 35 **Practicing academic vocabulary**

Briefly answer each of the questions.

1. What do you think is the most reliable source of information today? Why?

2. When someone asks you about your sleeping habits, what is your response?

3. Do you want to pursue a career in science? Explain.

4. What do you think dreams about money symbolize?

5. Which aspects of your sleeping habits are the most important to ensure that you get a good night's sleep?

6. Can you think of a dream that might indicate you are afraid of something?

7. When people interpret their dreams, what are they trying to do?

8. What are the most vital things that humans need for survival?

▷ **Assessing Your Learning at the End of a Chapter**

Revisiting Objectives

Return to the first page of this chapter. Think about the chapter objectives. Put a check mark next to the objectives you feel secure about. Review material in the chapter you still need to work on. When you are ready, answer the chapter review questions in Exercise 36.

▷ **Practicing for a Chapter Test**

EXERCISE 36 Reviewing comprehension

Check your comprehension of main concepts, or ideas, in this chapter by answering the following chapter review questions. First, write notes to answer the questions <u>without</u> looking back at the readings. Then, use the readings to check your answers and revise them, if necessary. Write your final answers in <u>complete sentences</u> on other paper.

1. In textbooks, what are *key terms*? Where do they often appear?
2. Which parts of your body undergo changes while you are sleeping?
3. What do the letters "REM" in *REM sleep* represent?
4. Is sleeping a *simple* process or a *complex* process? Briefly explain why.
5. According to Selection 2, what are the four theories that explain why people dream?
6. Do scientists have a clear explanation of the meaning of dreams? What are three scientific explanations for the meanings behind dreams?

EXERCISE 37 Defining *directive* words

Work with a partner. Read the sentences below, paying close attention to the bold-faced directive words. Match the directive word in each sentence with one of the meanings given in the box. Write the appropriate letter in the blank space. Discuss your answers with your classmates.

A. give the meaning of	**D.** to talk over, examine
B. to give an account of; to represent pictorially	**E.** sum up; give the main points briefly
C. to fix the value or worth of	**F.** to make plain or comprehensible

1. _____ **Summarize** the brain's activity during sleep.

2. _____ **Evaluate** Freud's theories about dreaming.

3. _____ **Explain** the stages of sleep.

4. _____ **Describe** what happens during hypnosis.

5. _____ **Define** the term *insomnia*.

6. _____ **Discuss** the use of electroencephalograms in sleep research.

EXERCISE 38 **Analyzing sample short-answer topics**

Study the sample short-answer questions in the boxes. Work with a partner.
For each question, do the following:

1. Underline the words in the question that indicate the main
   information the teacher is asking students to include in their
   answers.
2. Discuss how many sentences a student might have to write to
   answer the question completely.

Sample 1

In Selection 1, the writer says that sleeping is a complex
process. Explain two facts you learned from the reading that supports
the statement that sleeping is complex.

Sample 2

In Selection 1, the writer calls the last stages of sleep "active
sleep." Summarize why you think these stages are called active sleep.
Describe the activities that go on during these last stages of sleep.

Sample 3

In Selection 2, the writer says that according to Sigmund Freud,
dreams are "a way to satisfy unconscious desires or solve unconscious
problems." Define the term *unconscious desires*. Define the term
unconscious problems.

Sample 4

In Selection 3, the writer reports that, according to scientists,
dreams can be meaningless. They are simply the way our brains react
to the activities of our bodies during sleep. Evaluate this statement.

EXERCISE **39** **Answering short-answer questions**

Choose two of the sample questions above. Answer them in complete sentences. Pay attention to the directive words used in the questions. Be sure you answer the questions completely. After you finish, share your answers with your partner. Give each other suggestions about how to improve the answers.

Example Question and Short Answer

Q: In Selection 2, the writer says that dreams are logical. Define the term logical. Using information from the reading, explain how research has shown that dreams are logical.

A: When something is logical, it makes sense or seems reasonable. In Selection 2, the writer says that dreams are often logical. Researchers studied dreams that people had reported. They found that the events in the dreams usually followed a logical order. When other people were given a list of the events in these dreams, they could put them back in the correct, logical order. Also, research has shown that in reported dreams, people don't turn into objects, and objects don't turn into people. This also shows that dreams are logical.

Academic Vocabulary Review

To review the academic vocabulary words in this chapter, you will do a crossword puzzle.

Before you begin, look back at the academic words as they appear in the chapter reading selections. Remember the academic words are marked with dotted underlines. If there are words that you don't know, review the academic word exercises in the chapter.

Then, follow the steps in Exercise 40.

EXERCISE 40 **Crossword puzzle: Finding the clues**

Before you do the puzzle, read the sentences on the next page. Complete each sentence by writing in an academic word from the chapter. The words in the sentences are the clues for the puzzle that follows.

Across

3. A _____ is a set of steps that occur over and over in the same order.

4. During a _____ night of sleep, we go through six stages of sleep.

6. There are many _____ to explain why people dream.

8. Our daytime activities don't _____ our dreams at night very much.

10. Six stages of sleep _____ during a typical night's sleep.

11. When you are _____ of a dream as it is occurring, this is called lucid dreaming.

12. When a person hypnotizes others, he or she first asks the people to _____.

13. The _____ of a dream may vary from a few seconds to minutes or longer.

14. Doctors hook up a _____ to a person's head to show body actions in sleep.

Down

1. Doctors often study a person's dream to help treat the person's _____ problems.

2. Sleeping is a complex _____.

3. In _____ to quiet sleep, active sleep is the stage when people dream.

5. The _____ of the Jekyll and Hyde story is Robert Louis Stevenson.

7. Blind people dream, but their dreams usually don't contain _____ images.

9. In dreams, nonliving things don't usually _____ into living things.

EXERCISE 41 **Completing the puzzle**

Use the words in the sentences in Exercise 40 to complete the puzzle. Be sure to spell words correctly. Compare your answers with your classmates'.

Extensive Reading

Work with a partner or on your own to find out more about sleep and dreams. Choose one interesting paragraph or page from a book, a magazine, a newspaper, or an Internet source that relates to sleep or dreams.

Possible Topics of Readings

1. Sleep habits
2. Sleep problems, like insomnia
3. Sleeping pills
4. Meaning of dreams
5. Types of dreams
6. Hypnosis
7. Sleep walking

Go to a library and ask your librian to help you find an article or book. Photocopy the page with the paragraph or paragraphs that interest you.

Read the passage carefully. Write a one-paragraph summary of the passage. Be prepared to share your paragraph with classmates and explain the ideas in your reading.

You will hand in both your summary and photocopy to your instructor. If you work with a partner, each of you should write a separate summary and hand it in.

WEB POWER

Go to **elt.heinle.com/collegereading** to view
more readings on sleep and dreams, plus more exercises
that will help you study the Web readings and the
academic words in this chapter.

Women Speak Out

ACADEMIC FOCUS: LITERATURE AND WOMEN'S STUDIES

Academic Reading Objectives

After completing this chapter, you should be able to:

✓ Check here as you master each objective.

1. Know more vocabulary words used in your academic studies ☐
2. Recognize points in a writer's argument ☐
3. Identify various types of supporting ideas in a text ☐
4. Use context clues to guess the general meaning of unfamiliar words ☐
5. Read a lengthy text in manageable "chunks" to aid comprehension ☐
6. Draw conclusions from stated information ☐
7. Write a summary and reaction to a reading ☐

Literature and Women's Studies Objectives

1. Analyze general elements of literature ☐
2. Use historical and social background knowledge before reading literature ☐
3. Explain some key issues in women's studies ☐
4. Identify audience and purpose in literature ☐

Reading Assignment 1

LESSONS FOR WOMEN

▽ Getting Ready to Read

Focusing on Literature

EXERCISE 1 **Participating in class discussion**

Discuss the following questions with your classmates.

1. Study the definition of *literature* below:

   lit • er • a • ture *n.*   writing that is considered a form of art

   How does reading *literature* differ from other types of reading, like reading textbooks? Reading newspapers?

2. What topics do you expect to find in literature written by women? Explain why you think women are likely to write about these subjects.

3. Here are some names of well-known books and stories written by women. All of these stories were later made into movies. Circle the names you recognize. Do you know what the book is about? Do you know the name of the author (the writer)?

Frankenstein	*Joy Luck Club*	*Pride and Prejudice*
Little Women	*Harry Potter*	*Bridget Jones' Diary*
"The Birds"		

4. Do you know any other famous women writers of literature? If so, give their names and tell what you know about their writing.

5. One reading selection in this chapter is a *poem*. How does *poetry* differ from other kinds of writing? Do you think poems are more difficult to read than other types of writing? Why or why not?

6. Take a moment to reflect on the literature that you have read in your lifetime. Which stories do you remember? Why do they stay in your mind? Which types of literature do you like? Or, if you do not like reading literature, explain why.

Focusing on Literature: Historical and Social Background

STRATEGY

     In this chapter, you will read three selections of literature. It's useful to learn about the time in history and the society in which the piece of literature was written before you read it. This background information will help you better understand the meaning of the ideas in the literature.

EXERCISE 2   Reading titles and previewing information

Read the titles of the reading selections below. Think about the selections you will read.

Selections

1. "Lessons for Women"
2. "At Last Free"
3. "A Domestic Dilemma"

Discuss the following questions in your study group. Take notes on what your group members know. This will help prepare you to read.

1. Selection 1, "Lessons for Women," is an essay written by the most famous woman writer of ancient China. Pan Zhao lived from the years 45 to 117 CE (or AD).[1] She believed in the ideas of Confucius, the famous Chinese philosopher. Confucius taught that tradition keeps a society in order. Using this information, make a list of three "lessons for women" that you expect to find in this selection.

   a. _____

   b. _____

   c. _____

1. The term *CE* refers to years after the commonly accepted Year 1. *CE* refers to "common era." The term *BCE* refers to "before the common era." Other books may use the terms *BC* ("before Christ") or *AD* (*anno Domini*, "in the year of the Lord") instead of *BCE* and *CE*.

2. Selection 2, "At Last Free," is a poem written by a woman who lived in India in the sixth century BCE. Sumangalamata was the widow of a basket and sunshade maker, and she later became a Buddhist nun. From the title of the selection, what do you expect her to write about the life of women?

_____

_____

_____

_____

3. Selection 3 was written by Carson McCullers, a well-known American writer. Her story "A Domestic Dilemma" deals with a modern-day couple's relationship. What is a *dilemma*?

_____

_____

_____

4. What kinds of *dilemmas* do married couples face? Write your ideas in words, phrases, or sentences below.

_____

_____

_____

_____

_____

Focusing on Women's Studies: Exploring Key Women's Issues

The academic discipline of *women's studies* is growing in popularity at many colleges and universities. Students who major in women's studies commonly take courses across many disciplines, such as literature, history, science, social science, law, health, and education. The common threads that run throughout the courses are the *key issues* that affect women. *Issues* are subjects or problems that people discuss.

EXERCISE 3 **Participating in class discussion**

Discuss the following questions with your classmates:

1. What do you think are some *key issues* that specifically affect women?
2. At the University of Toronto's Institute for Women's Studies and Gender Studies, undergraduate (bachelor's degree) students take courses such as these:

   Gender, Race and Class in Contemporary Popular Culture
   Caribbean Women Writers
   Immigrant and Refugee Women
   Women and Health
   Gender Issues in Law
   Women and Issues of International Development

Read the names of the courses. Can you think of specific topics that might be included in each course? Which one(s) interest you? Explain.

3. If you judge from the course titles above, what are some key issues examined in a women's studies program?
4. Interestingly, few colleges and universities offer courses that might fall under a discipline you could call "Men's Studies." Why do you think "Women's Studies" programs are very popular, but few courses focus on men's issues?
5. Which courses would fit into a program that focused on "Men's Studies"? Make a list of possible courses on the lines below. Use the list in question 2 above as a guide.

   _____

   _____

   _____

   _____

   _____

   _____

6. Read the titles and descriptions of the Chapter 4 reading selections listed in Exercise 2. What key women's issues do you think these readings may explore?

▷ Reading for a Purpose

Guessing General Meanings of Unfamiliar Words

When you meet an unfamiliar word in reading, pay attention to the *context* of the word—that is, the words and sentences that come before and after the word. The context may give you clues to understanding an unfamiliar word. Research has shown that readers need to know almost all of the context words in order to guess the *precise meaning* of an unfamiliar word. Still, context clues help you get *general ideas* about an unfamiliar word.

Here are two ways to use the context of an unfamiliar word to give you *general ideas* about its meaning:

1. First, use the context to identify the part of speech and/or function of the unfamiliar word. Parts of speech include *noun, verb, adjective,* and *adverb.* The function of a word means how it is used in a sentence, such as *subject, verb,* or *object.* For example, in the sentence below, the word *neglected* is likely to be a *verb* because it follows a *subject* (or *noun*), the words *the natural order of things.*

   Subject (*n.*)   Verbs
   . . . the natural order of things are neglected and destroyed.

   This strategy works in nearly all sentences.

2. Next, use the surrounding words as clues to guess if the unfamiliar word has a *positive* or *negative* meaning. This strategy works in some sentences, not all.

   For instance, in the example phrase above, if you know the words *natural order* and *destroyed,* you can guess that the word *neglected* means something negative, like "ruined," "ignored," "disorganized," or "forgotten." In fact, *neglect* means "to pay little or no attention to someone or something, or to not take care of someone or something very well." It makes sense that the order of things "was not taken care of." The words *order of things* and *destroyed* are clues that help you guess the meaning of *neglected.*

EXERCISE 4 **Guessing general meanings of unfamiliar words**

Read the following sentences taken from Selection 1, "Lessons for Women," in the box below. Study the context of each bold-faced word. Then, in the right-hand column, write the word's part of speech on the line (n, v, adj, or adv). Put a check mark to show whether you think the word has a generally positive *or* negative *meaning, based on the context clues. Do not use a dictionary.*

The word in context	Part of speech and general meaning
Let a woman **yield** to others; let her respect others; let her put others first, herself last.	**yield** = _____ ____ positive meaning ____ negative meaning
To choose her words with care, to avoid **vulgar** language, to speak at appropriate times, and not to **weary** others with much conversation may be called the characteristics of womanly words.	**vulgar** = _____ ____ positive meaning ____ negative meaning **weary** = _____ ____ positive meaning ____ negative meaning
To wash and scrub **filth** away, to keep clothes and ornaments fresh and clean, to wash the head and bathe the body regularly, and to keep the person free from **disgraceful filth** may be called the characteristics of womanly bearing.	**filth** = _____ ____ positive meaning ____ negative meaning **disgraceful** = _____ ____ positive meaning ____ negative meaning
With **wholehearted devotion** to sew and to weave, to love not gossip and silly laughter, in cleanliness and order to prepare the wine and food for serving guests may be called the characteristics of womanly work.	**wholehearted** = _____ ____ positive meaning ____ negative meaning **devotion** = _____ ____ positive meaning ____ negative meaning

Now that you have determined the part of speech and negative or positive meaning of the unfamiliar words, guess the meaning of each bold-faced word. In the box below, check the meaning you think makes sense. Underline other words in the sentence that help you guess. Check your answers with a group of your classmates. Then use a dictionary to find precise meanings of each word.

The word in context . . .	. . . probably means _____.	
Let a woman **yield** to others; let her respect others; let her put others first, herself last.	**yield** to others ____ let herself be persuaded to others' ideas ____ control others ____ talk to others	
To choose her words with care, to avoid **vulgar** language, to speak at appropriate times, and not to **weary** others with much conversation may be called the characteristics of womanly words.	**vulgar** ____ sad ____ loud ____ rude	**weary** ____ relax ____ tire ____ anger
To wash and scrub **filth** away, to keep clothes and ornaments fresh and clean, to wash the head and bathe the body regularly, and to keep the person free from **disgraceful filth** may be called the characteristics of womanly bearing.	**filth** ____ dirt ____ clean ____ trouble	**disgraceful** ____ unclean ____ messy ____ unacceptable
With **wholehearted devotion** to sew and to weave, to love not gossip and silly laughter, in cleanliness and order to prepare the wine and food for serving guests may be called the characteristics of womanly work.	**wholehearted** ____ unwilling ____ enthusiastic ____ large	**devotion** ____ knowledge ____ violence ____ love

Text Organization

S T R A T E G Y

Argument Text Organization

In Chapters 1 and 2, you found that scientific texts are often organized into a series of theories and supporting ideas. This pattern of text organization is used in written arguments in general. An *argument* is a set of explanations a writer uses to prove that something is right or wrong or that something is true or false. An argument is usually organized with *points* followed by *support*.

Point ⟶ **Support**

The argument the writer wants reader to accept

Facts, examples, explanations to support argument

A *point* in an argument is a major idea the writer wants the reader to accept. *Support* refers to information the writer uses to show or prove that the point is correct. A writer may use examples, facts, or explanations to support a point. Like other types of major point sentences, sentences expressing an argumentative point may appear at the beginning of a paragraph.

Below is an example of the typical organization of an argument:

Point
One thing that a woman must learn is to accept her husband's decisions.

Support
A woman should never question the way her husband spends money, or where he goes when he is away from home.

EXERCISE 5 **Identifying points in an argument**

In Selection 1, "Lessons for Women," the writer makes an argument. As you read, focus on the points in the argument. Then, reread it and annotate the sentences that contain points. Do not annotate sentences that give examples, explanations, or other kinds of support.

Reading Selection 1

LESSONS FOR WOMEN

By Pan Zhao

CONFUCIUS
Le plus célèbre Philosophe de la Chine

Pan Zhao, the most famous woman writer in ancient China, believed in the teachings of Confucius.

Humility

1   Let a woman yield[1] to others; let her respect others; let her put others first, herself last. Should she do something good, let her not mention it; should she do something bad, let her not deny it. Let her endure[2] when others speak or do evil to her. Always let her seem to tremble and to fear. When a woman follows such rules as these, then she may be said to humble herself before others.

2   Let a woman retire late to bed, but rise early to duties; let her not dread[3] tasks by day or by night. Let her not refuse to perform domestic duties whether easy or difficult.

Husband and Wife

3   If a husband does not control his wife, then the rules of conduct manifesting[4] his authority are abandoned and broken. If a wife does not serve her husband, then the proper relationship between men and women and the natural order of things are neglected and destroyed.

Womanly Qualifications

4   A woman ought to have four qualifications: 1. womanly virtue,[5] 2. womanly words, 3. womanly bearing, and 4. womanly work. To guard her chastity,[6] to control her behavior, in every motion to exhibit modesty,[7] and to model each act on the best usage—this is womanly virtue.

1. *yield* = give way to pressure or superior authority from someone else
2. *endure* = to patiently suffer pain or a difficult situation for a long time
3. *dread* = to think of something in the future with dislike or fear
4. *manifesting* = making something easy to see; showing clearly
5. *virtue* = moral goodness of character and behavior
6. *chastity* = the state of not having sex with anyone
7. *modesty* = the quality of showing a moderate opinion about one's own talents, abilities, or accomplishments, or of not being showy in dress and behavior

5   To choose her words with care, to avoid vulgar language, to speak at appropriate times, and not to weary others with much conversation may be called the characteristics of womanly words.

6   To wash and scrub filth away, to keep clothes and ornaments fresh and clean, to wash the head and bathe the body regularly, and to keep the person free from disgraceful filth may be called the characteristics of womanly bearing.

7   With wholehearted devotion to sew and to weave, to love not gossip and silly laughter, in cleanliness and order to prepare the wine and food for serving guests may be called the characteristics of womanly work.

Source: From *Pan Chao: Foremost Woman Scholar of China, First Century A.D.: Background, Ancestry, Life, and Writings of the Most Celebrated Chinese Woman of Letters*, by Nancy Lee Swan, The Century Co., 1932. Copyright © The East Asian Library and the Gest Collection, Princeton University. Reprinted with permission.

▷ Assessing Your Learning

Demonstrating Comprehension

EXERCISE 6 Identifying the main idea

Read the four sentences below. Check the sentence that best expresses the main idea of the reading. Remember that the main idea should include the topic of the reading and what the writer says about the topic.

A. _____ The selection is about women's behavior.

B. _____ The selection gives lessons about how women should behave.

C. _____ The selection tells men to treat women like equals.

D. _____ The selection says that women should be humble.

Next, match each of the sentences above that you did not *choose with one of the following descriptions. Put the letter of the sentence next to the appropriate description. Share your answers with classmates.*

_____ This sentence is too general. It only tells what the reading is about.

_____ This sentence is too specific. It tells about only one idea in the reading.

_____ This sentence could be a main idea sentence, but it's untrue, according to the reading.

EXERCISE **7** **Identifying points in an argument**

Compare your annotations with a classmate's. Did you mark the same sentences? Discuss your answers, and then share your ideas with the rest of your class. Edit your annotations of this reading, if necessary.

EXERCISE **8** **Checking comprehension**

Check your understanding of ideas in the reading by marking the following statements true (T) or false (F). If a sentence is false, rewrite it to make it true. Discuss your answers with the rest of your class.

1. _____ According to the writer, a woman should think of her own needs before she thinks of other people's needs.

2. _____ A husband does not need to control his wife, the reading says.

3. _____ Speaking only at appropriate times is one example of "womanly virtue."

4. _____ A woman's *bearing* relates to her appearance.

5. _____ The reading suggests that it's bad for women to laugh too much.

EXERCISE **9** **Identifying audience and purpose**

Circle the best answer to the following questions about the audience and purpose of Selection 1. Compare your answers with your partner's.

1. The title of Selection 1 suggests that the <u>main</u> audience for the reading is
   A. women.
   B. men.

2. Circle the group or groups that may be part of the writer's audience.
   A. young, unmarried women
   B. old women
   C. young, unmarried men
   D. married men

3. In general, the purpose of this essay is to
   A. inform the reader.
   B. persuade the reader.

4. The specific purpose for which the writer wrote this essay was
   A. to help women become happier.
   B. to tell women how they should act.
   C. to tell women what will happen if they do not act correctly.

Master Student Tip

▼ **Audience and Purpose**

In writing, the audience means the readers, and purpose means the reason or reasons for writing something. A writer usually has one or more groups of readers in mind when he or she writes. Similarly, the writer may have one or more reasons for writing. Here are two general purposes for writing:

► To *inform* the reader—in other words, to give the reader information about a subject.

► To *persuade* the reader—that is, to make the reader believe something by giving good reasons.

Focusing on Women's Studies: Key Women's Issues

▼ **Summary and Reaction**

In many academic courses—in particular, literature courses—students commonly write a summary and reaction about a text. A summary and reaction should be organized with the following ideas:

▶ Begin with one or two sentences that introduce the text by title and author and state its main idea. (The title of a story, article, or essay should appear in quotation marks. The title of a book or film should be underlined or italicized.)

▶ Next, briefly state one or more of the reading's major points.

▶ Finally, explain your reaction to the reading as a whole and the major points you presented.

EXERCISE 10   Participating in group discussion

Discuss the following questions with your study group:

1. What is your reaction to the ideas in Selection 1, "Lessons for Women"?

2. Recall that this essay was written by a famous woman writer in ancient China. Judging from her ideas, what position, class, or role do you think she may have held in her society?

3. In modern times, which of her ideas would many women reject? Which ideas might some women agree with?

4. What types of women would agree with Zhao's ideas in "Lessons for Women"?

5. What types of men would agree with her ideas?

EXERCISE 11   Evaluating a summary and reaction

Read the paragraph-length summary-reaction below. You may not have read the book being summarized, but you can assume that the summary part of the paragraph is accurate. Discuss the questions that follow it with members of your study group.

Men Are from Mars, Women Are from Venus

Men Are from Mars, Women Are from Venus is a best-selling book written by psychologist Dr. John Gray. The title suggests the author's main point: that men and women have many differences. For example, two major points that Gray makes are that men don't share their feelings, while women are very emotional. In my opinion, the author is guilty of stereotyping and oversimplification. The statement that men do not express their feelings is a stereotype. Some men do share their feelings; others do not. Some women share their feelings, and others hold them in. Gray's views about men's unemotional behavior are oversimplified because, in fact, not all men are unemotional. Similarly, Gray describes women as being too emotional, which is also an oversimplified stereotype. Think about the women in your life. Are all of them overemotional? I would bet they were not. Most people know some women who cry a lot or show their fear or anger, but they also know women who are calm and hide their feelings. Gray's ideas are ridiculous because he makes broad generalizations and doesn't consider that people are individuals—both men and women. I say that some men are from Mars, and some women are, too. Some women are from Venus, and some men are, too.

▷ Questions for Discussion

1. Which sentences of the summary-reaction on page 135 give a summary of the original text? Underline and mark the one or more sentences that state the main idea of Gray's book. Underline and mark the one or more sentences that present Gray's major points.
2. Which sentences give the summary writer's reaction, or opinion?
3. What is the summary writer's overall opinion of Gray's book?
4. Assuming that the summary of Gray's book is accurate, do you agree or disagree with the summary writer's reaction? Explain.

EXERCISE 12 Writing a summary and reaction

Write a paragraph-length summary and reaction about Selection 1, "Lessons for Women." Begin with a sentence or sentences that state the title, author, and main idea of the reading. Then write sentences to summarize one or more major points in the reading. After that, write your reaction to the reading.

Example First Sentence of Summary and Reaction

The essay "Lessons for Women" by Pan zhao explains how women should behave.

▷ Learning Vocabulary

EXERCISE 13 Reviewing academic vocabulary

Put a check mark next to the academic vocabulary words from Selection 1 that you already know.

deny	authority	exhibit	devotion
conduct	abandon(ed)	usage	appropriate

Add unfamiliar words to your academic vocabulary list. For each unfamiliar word, write the word and its definition, and write a sentence using the word.

EXERCISE 14 Reviewing academic vocabulary

Use the academic vocabulary words in the box to complete the sentences below. Check your answers with a partner. Use a dictionary, if necessary.

| authority   exhibited   devote   appropriate   abandon   conduct |

"THE DUTIES OF WOMEN"

The ancient Hindu book *The Laws of Manu* described the duties of women in India long ago. The book presented strict rules of (1) _____ . First, women could never be independent. They had to live under the (2) _____ of men. A woman had to (3) _____ her life to her father, husband, or sons. A husband could take away his wife's property if she showed that she disliked him. Also, a husband could (4) _____ his wife if she was not able to have children. According to the laws, if a woman (5) _____ (6) _____ behavior, she would go to heaven.

Next, use each word to write a question about men's and women's roles in family, work, or society in general.

Example question:

> Do you think a man should have authority over a woman?

Ask a partner to answer your questions. Take turns asking and answering each other's questions.

Reading Assignment 2

AT LAST FREE

▷ Reading with a Purpose

As you read Selection 2, a poem titled "At Last Free," keep in mind the writer's *audience* and *purpose*. Think about the group or groups the writer is "speaking" to in her poem and the reasons why she is sharing her ideas.

Annotating the Text

Read the poem "At Last Free" and underline the most important ideas.

Buddhist nuns in Tilokpur, India

Reading Selection 2

AT LAST FREE

From *The Therigatha (Songs of the Nuns)*
Sumangalamata (sixth century BCE)

At last free,
at last I am a woman free!
No more tied to the kitchen,
amid the stained pots,
no more bound to the husband
who thought me less
than the shade he wove with his hands.
No more anger, no more hunger,
I sit now in the shade of my own tree.
Meditating thus, I am happy, serene.

Source: From *Women in Praise of the Sacred* by Jane Hirshfield, Editor. Copyright © 1994 by Jane Hirshfield. Reprinted by permission of HarperCollins Publishers, Inc.

▽ Assessing Your Learning

Demonstrating Comprehension

EXERCISE 15   Expressing the main idea

Write one sentence to express the main idea of Selection 2. In your main idea sentence, include the topic of the selection and the writer's idea, opinion, or attitude about it. Compare your sentence with a classmate's, and then share it with your class.

STRATEGY

Identifying Supporting Ideas

As you have learned, writers use *supporting ideas* in their writing to help show, explain, or prove main ideas and major points. In arguments, as well as in many other types of writing, *supporting ideas* may be examples, facts, explanations, or descriptive details.

Notice the major points and supporting ideas in this text, taken from Selection 1:

Major Points	Supporting Ideas (examples)
Let a woman modestly yield to others; let her respect others; let her put others first, herself last.	Should she do something good, let her not mention it; should she do something bad, let her not deny it.

EXERCISE 16   Identifying supporting ideas

Work with your partner to reread the poem. Circle lines of the poem that provide support (e.g., examples, explanations) about her main idea and major points. Share your answers with your class.

EXERCISE 17 Reviewing comprehension

With your partner, answer the following questions. Share your answers with your class. Write answers to the questions in complete sentences on another sheet of paper.

1. In the poem, the writer tells about two periods of her life. Whom do you think she lived with in the first part of her life? Identify the line or lines of the poem that give you this answer.
2. Who controls the writer's life in the second part of her life? Identify the line or lines of the poem that give you this answer.

Questions for Discussion

STRATEGY

Drawing Conclusions from Reading

A writer's ideas and opinions are not always stated directly. Often, the reader must make her or his own conclusions after reading. How can you do this? Use this three-step method:

1. Use the available information in the reading.
2. Use your own knowledge.
3. Consider all possibilities.

What conclusions can you draw about the relationship between the husband and wife based on the information stated below?

> *When her husband spoke to her, the woman looked down. Her eyes did not meet his. She did not speak. The man raised his arm to brush back his hair, and the woman quickly moved away from him.*

1. The available information in the reading tells us that "the woman looked down" and "did not speak" when her husband talked to her. Also, "the woman quickly moved away from him" when "the man raised his arm."

2. Our own knowledge tells us that husbands and wives may have good or bad relationships. Husbands and wives in bad relationships may abuse each other, verbally or physically.

3. There are many possibilities about the husband and wife's relationship. It's possible that they have a good relationship and that the husband and wife treat each other well. The opposite is also possible. Also, it's possible that their relationship is sometimes good and sometimes bad.

Conclusion: The husband and wife do not have a good relationship. The husband dominates the wife. The wife does not feel comfortable or safe with her husband.

EXERCISE 18 Drawing conclusions from reading

Work with a partner. Read each text given below. Use the three-step process to make a conclusion based on the information stated in the text. Below each text, write a sentence or sentences to express your conclusion. Share your answers with the class.

1. . . . no more bound to the husband

   who thought me less

   than the shade he wove with his hands.

   Conclusion: _____

   _____

   _____

2. No more anger, no more hunger,

   I sit now in the shade of my own tree.

   Meditating thus, I am happy, serene.

   Conclusion: _____

   _____

   _____

EXERCISE 19 Drawing conclusions about a reading

Using the conclusions you made in Exercise 18 above, write one or two sentences to state your general conclusions about the couple in the poem. What kind of relationship did they have? Was it successful? According to the wife, did they have problems? Answer these questions with one or two sentences. Share your conclusion in your study group.

EXERCISE 20 Writing a summary and reaction

Write a paragraph-length summary and reaction to "At Last Free," Selection 2. Use the information in the poem to write the summary part of your paragraph, and use the conclusions you have drawn about the poem to write the reaction part.

▷ Linking Concepts

Focusing on Women's Studies: Key Women's Issues

EXERCISE 21 Transferring ideas to personal experience

Discuss the questions below with a group of your classmates.

1. Do you have any personal experience with husband-and-wife relationships like the one described in Selection 2? If so, describe the situation.
2. In your experience, do you know a woman or women who obey the rules stated in "Lessons for Women," Selection 1? Which of the rules do the women follow? Describe their situations.

▷ Reading Journal

In Selection 2, "At Last Free," written in the sixth century BCE, the writer presented negative ideas about married life. Do you think she had good reasons for describing her marriage in a negative way? Do her opinions about marriage seem old-fashioned or modern? Answer these questions in a one-page journal entry. Use information from the poem to support your ideas.

Reading Assignment 3

A DOMESTIC DILEMMA

▷ **Reading for a Purpose**

EXERCISE 22 Guessing meanings of unfamiliar words

Read the passages in the box below, taken from Selection 3, "A Domestic Dilemma." Write each word's part of speech (n, v, adj, or adv) on the line next to the word. Then, check the appropriate box to indicate if you think the word has a positive or a negative meaning.

The word in context	Part of speech and general meaning
This evening Martin kept his face close to the window and watched the **barren** fields and lonely lights of passing townships. There was a moon, pale on the dark earth and areas of late, porous snow; to Martin the countryside seemed vast and somehow **desolate** that evening.	**barren** = _____ ____ positive meaning ____ negative meaning **desolate** = _____ ____ positive meaning ____ negative meaning
As she went into the bathroom Emily walked with careful gravity. She turned on the cold water and dashed some on her face with her cupped hands, then patted herself dry with the corner of a bath towel. Her face was **delicately** featured and young, **unblemished**.	**delicately** = _____ ____ positive meaning ____ negative meaning **unblemished** = _____ ____ positive meaning ____ negative meaning
The baby had been dropped, her **frail**, frail skull striking the table edge, so that a thread of blood was soaking into the **gossamer** child, so infinitely precious at that moment, he had an affrighted vision of the future.	**frail** = _____ ____ positive meaning ____ negative meaning **gossamer** = _____ ____ positive meaning ____ negative meaning

Use the context clues to help you guess the meaning of each bold-faced word. In the box below, put a check mark next to the meaning you think makes sense. Underline other words in the sentence that help you guess. Compare your answers with a classmate's, and then check your answers with a dictionary.

The word in context . . .	. . . probably means _____.	
This evening Martin kept his face close to the window and watched the **barren** fields and lonely lights of passing townships. There was a moon, pale on the dark earth and areas of late, porous snow; to Martin the countryside seemed vast and somehow **desolate** that evening.	**barren** ____ fertile ____ productive ____ unproductive	**desolate** ____ lively ____ attractive ____ empty
As she went into the bathroom Emily walked with careful gravity. She turned on the cold water and dashed some on her face with her cupped hands, then patted herself dry with the corner of a bath towel. Her face was **delicately** featured and young, **unblemished**.	**delicately** ____ gracefully ____ unattractively ____ carelessly	**unblemished** ____ unhappy ____ clear ____ wrinkled
The baby had been dropped, her **frail**, frail skull striking the table edge, so that a thread of blood was soaking into the **gossamer** child, so infinitely precious at that moment, he had an affrighted vision of the future.	**frail** ____ strong ____ weak ____ beautiful	**gossamer** ____ strong ____ delicate ____ tough

STRATEGY

Reading a Lengthy Text in "Chunks"

When a reading selection is lengthy, divide it into "chunks," or sections, and read one part at a time. Stop after each section to self-check your understanding. This will help you understand the entire reading and remember its ideas more clearly.

EXERCISE 23   Reading a text by sections

Read section 1 of Selection 3 once without a dictionary. Highlight or underline important ideas. Then, self-check your comprehension by answering the questions after the section. Reread section 1 as many times as necessary, looking up unfamiliar words in the dictionary. Do the same when you read sections 2 and 3.

Reading Selection 3

A DOMESTIC DILEMMA

By Carson McCullers

Section 1

1   On Thursday Martin Meadows left the office early enough to make the first express bus home. It was the hour when the evening lilac glow was fading in the slushy streets, but by the time the bus had left the Mid-town terminal the bright city night had come. On Thursdays the maid had a half-day off and Martin liked to get home

as soon as possible, since for the past year his wife had not been—well. This Thursday he was very tired and, hoping that no regular commuter would single him out for conversation, he fastened his attention to the newspaper until the bus had crossed the George Washington Bridge. Once on 9-W Highway Martin always felt that the trip was halfway done, he breathed deeply, even in cold weather when only ribbons of draught cut through the smoky air of the bus, confident that he was breathing country air. It used to be that at this point he would relax and begin to think with pleasure of his home. But in this last year nearness brought only a sense of tension and he did not anticipate the journey's end. This evening Martin kept his face close to the window and watched the barren fields and lonely lights of passing townships. There was a moon, pale on the dark earth and areas of late, porous snow; to Martin the countryside seemed vast and somehow desolate that evening. He took his hat from the rack and put his folded newspaper in the pocket of his overcoat a few minutes before time to pull the cord.

2   The cottage was a block from the bus stop, near the river but not directly on the shore; from the living-room window you could look across the street and opposite yard and see the Hudson. The cottage was modern, almost too white and new on the narrow plot of yard. In summer the grass was soft and bright and Martin carefully tended a flower border and a rose trellis. But during the cold, fallow[1] months the yard was bleak and the cottage seemed naked. Lights were on that evening in all the rooms in the little house and Martin hurried up the front walk. Before the steps he stopped to move a wagon out of the way.

3   The children were in the living room, so intent on play that the opening of the front door was at first unnoticed. Martin stood looking at his safe, lovely children. They had opened the bottom drawer of the secretary and taken out the Christmas decorations. Andy had managed to plug in the Christmas tree lights and the green and red bulbs glowed with out-of-season festivity on the rug of the living room. At the moment he was trying to trail the bright cord over Marianne's rocking horse. Marianne sat on the floor pulling off an angel's wings. The children wailed a startling welcome. Martin swung the fat little baby girl up to his shoulder and Andy threw himself against his father's legs.

1. *fallow* = unproductive

4   "Daddy, Daddy, Daddy!"

5   Martin set down the little girl carefully and swung Andy a few times like a pendulum.[2] Then he picked up the Christmas tree cord.

6   "What's all this stuff doing out? Help me put it back in the drawer. You're not to fool with the light socket. Remember I told you that before. I mean it, Andy."

7   The six-year-old child nodded and shut the secretary drawer. Martin stroked his fair soft hair and his hand lingered tenderly on the nape of the child's frail neck.

8   "Had supper yet, Bumpkin?"

9   "It hurt. The toast was hot."

10   The baby girl stumbled on the rug and, after the first surprise of the fall, began to cry; Martin picked her up and carried her in his arms back to the kitchen.

11   "See, Daddy," said Andy. "The toast—"

12   Emily had laid the children's supper on the uncovered porcelain table. There were two plates with the remains of cream-of-wheat and eggs and silver mugs that had held milk. There was also a platter of cinnamon toast, untouched except for one tooth-marked bite. Martin sniffed the bitten piece and nibbled gingerly. Then he put the toast into the garbage pail.

13   "Hoo—phui—What on earth!"

14   Emily had mistaken the tin of cayenne[3] for the cinnamon.

15   "I like to have burnt up," Andy said. "Drank water and ran outdoors and opened my mouth. Marianne didn't eat none."

16   "Any," corrected Martin. He stood helpless, looking around the walls of the kitchen. "Well, that's that, I guess," he said finally. "Where is your mother now?"

17   "She's up in you all's room."

18   Martin left the children in the kitchen and went up to his wife. Outside the door he waited for a moment to still his anger. He did not knock and once inside the room he closed the door behind him.

End of Section 1

---

2. *pendulum* = a weight hung from a fixed support so that it swings freely, often used to regulate the action of clocks

3. *cayenne* = a very strong-sharp-tasting seasoning made from the ground pods of red peppers

EXERCISE **24** **Self-checking your comprehension**

Fill in the missing information in the following sentences to check your understanding of section 1. Reread the section, if necessary, to clarify your understanding. When you can answer all the questions easily, move to section 2.

1. Martin was traveling from his _____ to his

   _____ . (*Note:* You don't need to give specific

   names of places.)

2. Martin was feeling _____ as he traveled.

3. Marianne and Andy were the names of Martin's _____.

4. When Martin arrived, Marianne and Andy were _____

   _____.

5. Emily was the children's _____ and Martin's

   _____.

6. When Martin arrived, Emily was in _____.

Section 2

19   Emily sat in the rocking chair by the window of the pleasant room. She had been drinking something from a tumbler and as he entered she put the glass hurriedly on the floor behind the chair. In her <u>attitude</u> there was confusion and guilt which she tried to hide by a show of spurious[4] vivacity.[5]

20   "Oh, Marty! You home already? The time slipped up on me. I was just going down—" She lurched to him and her kiss was strong with sherry.[6] When he stood <u>unresponsive</u> she stepped back a pace and giggled nervously.

21   "What's the matter with you? Standing there like a barber pole. Is anything wrong with you?"

22   "Wrong with *me*?" Martin bent over the rocking chair and picked up the tumbler from the floor. "If you could only realize how sick I am—how bad it is for all of us."

4. *spurious* = false, not genuine
5. *vivacity* = liveliness
6. *sherry* = alcoholic drink

23   Emily spoke in a false, airy voice that had become too familiar to him. Often at such times she affected a slight English accent, copying perhaps some actress she admired. "I haven't the vaguest idea what you mean. Unless you are referring to the glass I used for a spot of sherry. I had a finger of sherry—maybe two. But what is the crime in that, pray tell me? I'm quite all right. Quite all right."

24   "So anyone can see."

25   As she went into the bathroom Emily walked with careful gravity.[7] She turned on the cold water and dashed some on her face with her cupped hands, then patted herself dry with the corner of a bath towel. Her face was delicately featured and young, unblemished.

26   "I was just going down to make dinner." She tottered and balanced herself by holding to the door frame.

27   "I'll take care of dinner. You stay up here. I'll bring it up."

28   "I'll doing nothing of the sort. Why, whoever heard of such a thing?"

29   "Please," Martin said.

30   "Leave me alone. I'm quite all right. I was just on the way down—"

31   "Mind what I say."

32   "Mind your grandmother."

33   She lurched toward the door, but Martin caught her by the arm. "I don't want the children to see you in this condition. Be reasonable."

34   "Condition!" Emily jerked her arm. Her voice rose angrily. "Why, because I drink a couple of sherries in the afternoon you're trying to make me out a drunkard. Condition! Why, I don't even touch whiskey. As well you know. *I* don't swill liquor at bars. And that's more than you can say. I don't even have a cocktail at dinnertime. I only sometimes have a glass of sherry. What, I ask you, is the disgrace of that? Condition!"

35   Martin sought words to calm his wife. "We'll have a quiet supper by ourselves up here. That's a good girl." Emily sat on the side of the bed and he opened the door for a quick departure.

36   "I'll be back in a jiffy."

37   As he busied himself with the dinner downstairs he was lost in the familiar question as to how this problem had come upon his house. He himself had always enjoyed a good drink. When they were still living in Alabama they had served long drinks or cocktails as a matter of course. For years they had drunk one or two—possibly

7. *gravity* = seriousness

three drinks before dinner, and at bedtime a long nightcap. Evenings before holidays they might get a buzz on, might even become a little tight.[8] But alcohol had never seemed a problem to him, only a bothersome expense that with the increase in the family they could scarcely afford. It was only after his company had transferred him to New York that Martin was aware that certainly his wife was drinking too much. She was tippling, he noticed, during the day.

38   The problem acknowledged, he tried to analyze the source. The change from Alabama to New York had somehow disturbed her; accustomed to the idle warmth of a small Southern town, the matrix[9] of the family and cousinship and childhood friends, she had failed to accommodate herself to the stricter, lonelier mores of the North. The duties of motherhood and housekeeping were onerous to her. Homesick for Paris City, she had made no friends in the suburban town. She read only magazines and murder books. Her interior life was insufficient without the artifice[10] of alcohol.

39   The revelations of incontinence insidiously undermined his previous conceptions of his wife. There were times of unexplainable malevolence, times when the alcoholic fuse caused an explosion of unseemly anger. He encountered a latent coarseness in Emily, inconsistent with her natural simplicity. She lied about drinking and deceived him with unsuspected stratagems.

40   Then there was an accident. Coming home from work one evening about a year ago, he was greeted with screams from the children's room. He found Emily holding the baby, wet and naked from her bath. The baby had been dropped, her frail, frail skull striking the table edge, so that a thread of blood was soaking into the gossamer child, so infinitely precious at that moment, he had an affrighted vision of the future.

41   The next day Marianne was all right. Emily vowed that never again would she touch liquor, and for a few weeks she was sober, cold and downcast. Then gradually she began—not whiskey or gin—but quantities of beer, or sherry, or outlandish liqueurs; once he had come across a hatbox of empty crème de menthe bottles. Martin found a dependable maid who managed the household competently.

---

8. *To get a buzz on* and *become a little tight* are slang expressions for getting drunk.
9. *matrix* = a situation within which something else originates, develops or is contained
10. *artifice* = trickery, strategy

Virgie was also from Alabama and Martin had never dared tell Emily the wage scale customary in New York. Emily's drinking was entirely secret now, done before he reached the house. Usually the effects were almost imperceptible[11]—a looseness of movement or the heavy-lidded eyes. The times of irresponsibilities, such as the cayenne-pepper toast were rare, and Martin could dismiss his worries when Virgie was at the house. But, <u>nevertheless</u>, anxiety was always latent, a threat of indefined disaster that underlaid his days.

End of Section 2

EXERCISE 25 Self-checking your comprehension

Fill in the missing information in the following sentences to check your understanding of section 2. Reread the section, using a dictionary, if necessary. When you can answer all the questions easily, move to section 3.

1. Emily was drinking _____ when Martin got home.

2. Martin's family moved from _____ to New York because _____.

3. Martin thought his wife drank because _____.

4. In the accident described in this section, the baby _____

    _____.

5. Virgie was the family's _____.

Section 3

42   "Marianne!" Martin called, for even the recollection of that time brought the need for reassurance. The baby girl, no longer hurt, but no less precious to her father, came into the kitchen with her brother. Martin went on with the preparations for the meal. He opened a can of soup and put two chops in the frying pan. Then he sat down by the table and took his Marianne on his knees for a pony ride. Andy watched them, his fingers wobbling the tooth that had been loose all that week.

11. *imperceptible* = undetectable, not noticeable or visible

43   "Andy-the-candyman!" Martin said. "Is that old critter still in your mouth? Come closer, let Daddy have a look."

44   "I got a string to pull it with." The child brought from his pocket a tangled thread. "Virgie said to tie it to the tooth and tie the other end to the doorknob and shut the door real suddenly."

45   Martin took out a clean handkerchief and felt the loose tooth carefully. "That tooth is coming out of my Andy's mouth tonight. Otherwise I'm awfully afraid we'll have a tooth tree in the family."

46   "A what?"

47   "A tooth tree," Martin said. "You'll bite into something and swallow that tooth. And the tooth will take root in poor Andy's stomach and grow into a tooth tree with sharp little teeth instead of leaves."

48   "Shoo, Daddy," Andy said. But he held the tooth firmly between his grimy little thumb and forefinger. "There ain't any tree like that. I never seen one."

49   "There *isn't* any tree like that and I never *saw* one."

50   Martin tensed suddenly. Emily was coming down the stairs. He listened to the fumbling footsteps, his arm embracing the little boy with dread. When Emily came into the room he saw from her movements and her sullen[12] face that she had again been at the sherry bottle. She began to yank open drawers and set the table.

51   "Condition!" she said in a furry voice. "You talk to me like that. Don't think I'll forget. I remember every dirty lie you say to me. Don't you think for a minute that I forget."

52   "Emily!" he begged. "The children—"

53   "The children—yes! Don't think I don't see through your dirty plots and schemes. Down here trying to turn my own children against me. Don't think I don't see and understand."

54   "Emily! I beg you—please go upstairs."

55   "So you can turn my children—my very own children—" Two large tears coursed rapidly down her cheeks. "Trying to turn my little boy, my Andy, against his own mother."

56   With drunken impulsiveness[13] Emily knelt on the floor before the startled child. Her hands on his shoulders balanced her. "Listen, my Andy—you wouldn't listen to any lies your father tells you? You wouldn't believe what he says? Listen, Andy, what was your father telling you before I came downstairs?" Uncertain, the child sought his father's face. "Tell me. Mama wants to know."

12. *sullen* = irritable
13. *impulsiveness* = tendency to act without planning or thinking

57   "About the tooth tree."

58   "What?"

59   The child repeated the words and she echoed them with unbelieving terror. "The tooth tree!" She swayed and renewed her grasp on the child's shoulder. "I don't know what you're talking about. But listen, Andy, Mama is all right, isn't she?" The tears were spilling down her face and Andy drew back from her, for he was afraid. Grasping the table edge, Emily stood up.

60   "See! You have turned my child against me."

61   Marianne began to cry, and Martin took her in his arms.

62   "That's all right, you can take *your* child. You have always shown partiality from the very first. I don't mind, but at least you can leave me my little boy."

63   Andy edged close to his father and touched his leg. "Daddy," he wailed.

64   Martin took the children to the foot of the stairs. "Andy, you take up Marianne and Daddy will follow you in a minute."

65   "But Mama?" the child asked, whispering.

66   "Mama will be all right. Don't worry."

67   Emily was sobbing at the kitchen table, her face buried in the crook of her arm. Martin poured a cup of soup and set it before her. Her rasping sobs unnerved him; the vehemence of her emotion, irrespective of[14] the source, touched in him a strain of tenderness. Unwillingly he laid his hand on her dark hair. "Sit up and drink the soup." Her face as she looked up at him was chastened[15] and imploring. The boy's withdrawal or the touch of Martin's hand had turned the tenor[16] of her mood.

68   "Ma-Martin," she sobbed. "I'm so ashamed."

69   "Drink the soup."

70   Obeying him, she drank between gasping breaths. After a second cup she allowed him to lead her up to their room. She was docile now and more restrained. He laid her nightgown on the bed and was about to leave the room when a fresh round of grief, the alcoholic tumult,[17] came again.

---

14. *irrespective of* = regardless of
15. *chastened* = corrected by punishment; restrained
16. *tenor* = the course of thought running through something written or spoken
17. *tumult* = disturbance of the mind or emotions

71   "He turned away. My Andy looked at me and turned away."

72   Impatience and fatigue hardened his voice, but he spoke warily. "You forget that Andy is still a little child—he can't comprehend the meaning of such scenes."

73   "Did I make a scene? Oh, Martin, did I make a scene before the children?"

74   Her horrified face touched and amused him against his will. "Forget it. Put on your nightgown and go to sleep."

75   "My child turned away from me. Andy looked at his mother and turned away. The children—"

76   She was caught in the rhythmic sorrow of alcohol. Martin withdrew from the room saying: "For God's sake go to sleep. The children will forget by tomorrow."

77   As he said this he wondered if it was true. Would the scene glide so easily from memory—or would it root in the unconscious to fester in the after-years? Martin did not know, and the last alternative sickened him. He thought of Emily, foresaw the morning-after humiliation: the shards[18] of memory, the lucidities[19] that glared from the obliterating[20] darkness of shame. She would call the New York office twice—possibly three or four times. Martin anticipated his own embarrassment, wondering if the others at the office could possibly suspect. He felt that his secretary had divined[21] the trouble long ago and that she pitied him. He suffered a moment of rebellion against his fate; he hated his wife.

78   Once in the children's room he closed the door and felt secure for the first time that evening. Marianne fell down on the floor, picked herself up and calling: "Daddy, watch me," fell again, got up, and continued the falling-calling routine. Andy sat in the child's low chair, wobbling the tooth. Martin ran the water in the tub, washed his own hands in the lavatory, and called the boy into the bathroom.

79   "Let's have another look at that tooth." Martin sat on the toilet, holding Andy between his knees. The child's mouth gaped and Martin grasped the tooth. A wobble, a quick twist and the nacreous[22] milk tooth was free. Andy's face was for the moment split between terror, astonishment, and delight. He mouthed a swallow of water and spat into the lavatory.

18. *shards* = broken pieces
19. *lucidities* = state of being mentally sound; sanity
20. *obliterating* = removing
21. *divined* = guessed
22. *nacreous* = having an iridescent, or rainbowlike, color

80   "Look, Daddy! It's blood. Marianne!"

81   Martin loved to bathe his children, loved inexpressibly the tender, naked bodies as they stood in the water so exposed. It was not fair of Emily to say that he showed partiality. As Martin soaped the delicate boy-body of his son he felt that further love would be impossible. Yet he admitted the difference in the quality of his emotions for the two children. His love for his daughter was graver, touched with a strain of melancholy, a gentleness that was akin to[23] pain. His pet names for the little boy were the absurdities[24] of daily inspiration—he called the little girl always Marianne, and his voice as he spoke it was a caress. Martin patted dry the fat baby stomach and the sweet little genital[25] fold. The washed child faces were radiant as flower petals, equally loved.

82   "I'm putting the tooth under my pillow. I'm supposed to get a quarter."

83   "What for?"

84   "*You* know, Daddy. Johnny got a quarter for his tooth."

85   "Who puts the quarter there?" asked Martin. "I used to think fairies left it in the night. It was a dime in my day, though."

86   "That's what they say in kindergarten."

87   "Who does put it there?"

88   "Your parents," Andy said. "You!"

89   Martin pinned the cover on Marianne's bed. His daughter was already asleep. Scarcely breathing, Martin bent over and kissed her forehead, kissed again the tiny hand that lay palm-upward, flung in slumber beside her head.

90   "Good night, Andy-man."

91   The answer was only a drowsy murmur. After a minute Martin took out his change and slid a quarter underneath the pillow. He left a night light in the room.

92   As Martin prowled about the kitchen making a late meal, it occurred to him that the children had not once mentioned their mother or the scene that must have seemed to them incomprehensible. Absorbed in the instant—the tooth, the bath, the quarter—the fluid passage of child-time had borne these weightless episodes like leaves in the swift current of a shallow stream while the adult enigma was beached and forgotten on the shore. Martin thanked the Lord for that.

23. *akin to* = similar to
24. *absurdities* = ridiculous conditions or states
25. *genital* = relating to the external sexual organs

93   But his own anger, repressed and lurking,[26] arose again. His youth was being frittered by a drunkard's waste, his very manhood subtly undermined. And the children, once the immunity[27] of incomprehension passed—what would it be like in a year or so? With his elbows on the table he ate his food brutishly, untasting. There were no hiding the truth—soon there would be gossip in the office and in the town; his wife was a dissolute[28] woman. Dissolute. And he and his children were bound to a future of degradation[29] and slow ruin.

94   Martin pushed away from the table and stalked into the living room. He followed the lines of a book with his eyes but his mind conjured miserable images: he saw his children drowned in the river, his wife a disgrace on the public street. By bedtime the dull, hard anger was like a weight upon his chest and his feet dragged as he climbed the stairs.

95   The room was dark except for the shafting light from the half-opened bathroom door. Martin undressed quietly. Little by little, peaceful respiration sounded gently in the room. Her high-heeled shoes with the carelessly dropped stockings made to him a mute[30] appeal. Her underclothes were flung in disorder on the chair. Martin picked up the girdle and the soft-silk brassiere and stood for a moment with them in his hands. For the first time that evening he looked at his wife. His eyes rested on the sweet forehead, the arch of the fine brow. The brow had descended to Marianne, and the tilt at the end of the delicate nose. In his son he could trace the high cheekbones and pointed chin. Her body was full-bosomed, slender and undulant.[31] As Martin watched the tranquil slumber of his wife the ghost of the old anger vanished. All thoughts of blame or blemish were distant from him now. Martin put out the bathroom light and raised the window. Careful not to awaken Emily he slid into the bed. By moonlight he watched his wife for the last time. His hand sought the adjacent flesh and sorrow paralleled desire in the immense complexity of love.

End Section 3

26. *lurking* = lying in wait; sneaking
27. *immunity* = protection
28. *dissolute* = lacking moral restraint; indulging in sensual pleasures or vices
29. *degradation* = state of having one's honor or dignity lowered
30. *mute* = silent
31. *undulant* = moving smoothly, like ocean waves

▷ Assessing Your Learning

Demonstrating Comprehension

EXERCISE 26 Self-checking your comprehension

*Fill in the missing information in the following sentences to check your
understanding of section 3 of the story. Reread the section as necessary to
complete the sentences. When you think you can answer all the questions
easily, continue with the next exercise to check your comprehension of the
entire story.*

1. In this part of the story, Martin helped to remove his son's _____ .

2. Emily came downstairs and asked Andy to tell her _____
   _____ .

3. The children started to cry, so Martin asked Andy to take his sister
   _____ .

4. Emily felt _____ after the children go to bed.

5. She ate _____ , and then she _____
   _____ .

6. Before the children went to sleep, Martin went to their room and
   _____ in the bathroom.

7. Then, Martin saw his wife in _____ and finally went to sleep.

EXERCISE 27 **Checking comprehension of the entire story**

Check your understanding of ideas in Selection 3, "A Domestic Dilemma," by putting the following events in the correct order as they occurred in the story. Write "1" next to the first event, "2" next to the second event, and so on.

1. _____ Marianne started to cry.

2. _____ Martin rode home on the bus.

3. _____ His wife Emily told him that she didn't realize the time.

4. _____ Martin made a late meal and then tried to read.

5. _____ Marianne and Andy were playing in the living room.

6. _____ Martin made Emily eat some soup.

7. _____ Martin bathed his children.

8. _____ Emily felt ashamed that she had made the children cry.

9. _____ Martin bathed his children and puts them to bed.

10. _____ Andy helped his sister go upstairs.

After you have ordered the events, check your answers with a partner or in your study group. If you have different answers, scan the reading to find each event that is expressed in the sentences above. Write the page number and paragraph number next to each sentence.

Discuss your answers with the rest of your class.

In your study group or with your partner, use the ten sentences to write a short summary of the reading. Begin your summary with a main idea sentence that contains the title of the story, the author, and a brief phrase telling what the story is about. Share your summary with the rest of your class.

EXERCISE 28 **Checking comprehension**

Read the sentences in the left-hand column of the chart below, which are taken from Selection 3, "A Domestic Dilemma." For each sentence, put a check mark next to the sentence on the right with the same or similar meaning. Discuss your answer with your study group members.

1. The children were in the living room, so intent on play that the opening of the front door was at first unnoticed. (¶ 3)	The children didn't see when their father came in the door.
	The children opened the front door to let their father in.
2. Emily sat in the rocking chair by the window of the pleasant room. She had been drinking something from a tumbler and as he entered she put the glass hurriedly on the floor behind the chair. In her attitude there there was confusion and guilt which she tried to hide by a show of spurious vivacity. (¶ 20)	Emily tried to cover her drink when her husband came in the room.
	Emily was sitting in a chair looking happy when her husband walked in.
3. The change from Alabama to New York had somehow disturbed her; accustomed to the idle warmth of a small Southern town, the matrix of the family and cousinship and childhood friends, she had failed to accommodate herself to the stricter, lonelier mores of the North. (¶ 39)	Emily preferred living in the North to living in the South.
	Emily did not adjust well to living in the North.
4. Emily vowed that never again would she touch liquor, and for a few weeks she was sober, cold and downcast. (¶ 42)	Emily was happy that she had decided not to drink anymore.
	Emily promised not to drink, but not drinking made her sad.

5. … Martin could dismiss his worries when Virgie was at the house. But, nevertheless, anxiety was always latent, a threat of undefined disaster that underlaid his days. (¶ 42)	Even though Martin didn't worry when Virgie was home, he still worried that something bad would happen.
	Martin was carefree now that he had hired Virgie as his housekeeper.
6. Her rasping sobs unnerved him; the vehemence of her emotion, irrespective of the source, touched in him a strain of tenderness. (¶ 69)	Martin felt sorry for Emily because she was crying.
	Martin was angry that Emily showed such emotion.
7. Would the scene glide so easily from memory—or would it root in the unconscious to fester in the after-years? Martin did not know, and the last alternative sickened him. (¶ 78)	Martin was certain that his children would long remember the drunkenness of their mother.
	Martin was upset because he thought the children might recall Emily's drunken scene.
8. As Martin soaped the delicate boy-body of his son he felt that further love would be impossible. (¶ 83)	Martin didn't think that he could love his son, Andy, any longer.
	Martin didn't think that he could love his son, Andy, more than he did.
9. … it occurred to him that the children had not not once mentioned their mother or the scene that must have seemed to them incomprehensible. Absorbed in the instant— the tooth, the bath, the quarter—the fluid passage of child-time had borne these weightless episodes like leaves in the swift current of a shallow stream … Martin thanked the Lord for that. (¶ 94)	Martin was afraid that the children would remember the scene with their mother.
	Martin was happy that the children didn't seem to remember the scene with their mother.

▽ Questions for Discussion

EXERCISE 29   **Drawing conclusions from reading**

Read each passage from Selection 3 below, and make a conclusion based on the information stated. Go back to the story, find the sentences, and see how they fit into the story. Use the three-step process identified on page 140. Below each text, write a sentence or sentences to express your conclusion. Share your answers with the class.

1. It used to be that at this point he would relax and begin to think with pleasure of his home. But in this last year nearness brought only a sense of tension and he did not anticipate the journey's end. (¶ 1)

   Conclusion: _____

   _____

   _____

2. The children wailed a startling welcome. Martin swung the fat little baby girl up to his shoulder and Andy threw himself against his father's legs.
   "Daddy, Daddy, Daddy!" (¶ 3–4)

   Conclusion: _____

   _____

   _____

3. Martin stroked his fair soft hair and his hand lingered tenderly on the nape of the child's frail neck. (¶ 7)

   Conclusion: _____

   _____

   _____

4. She had been drinking something from a tumbler and as he entered she put the glass hurriedly on the floor behind the chair. In her attitude there was confusion and guilt which she tried to hide . . . (¶ 19)

   Conclusion: _____

   _____

   _____

5. "I was just going down to make dinner." She tottered and balanced herself by holding to the door frame. (¶ 27)

   Conclusion: _____

   _____

   _____

6. Martin tensed suddenly. Emily was coming down the stairs. He listened to the fumbling footsteps, his arm embracing the little boy with dread. (¶ 51)

   Conclusion: _____

   _____

   _____

7. "That's all right, you can take *your* child. You have always shown partiality from the very first. I don't mind, but at least you can leave me my little boy." (¶ 64)

   Conclusion: _____

   _____

   _____

8. … his [Martin's] mind conjured miserable images: he saw his children drowned in the river, his wife a disgrace on the public street. (¶ 96)

   Conclusion: _____

   _____

   _____

9. By moonlight he watched his wife for the last time. His hand sought the adjacent flesh and sorrow paralleled desire in the immense complexity of love. (¶ 95)

   Conclusion: _____

   _____

   _____

EXERCISE 30   **Writing a summary-reaction**

Write two summary and reaction paragraphs about Selection 3, "A Domestic Dilemma." First, write one summary paragraph to briefly introduce the family members, describe their situation, and relate the main events that occur in the story. Use the short summary that you wrote on page 158. Just add the names of family members, their relationships, and their situation, if you do not include them. Do not include your opinions in this paragraph. Then, using the conclusions you made in Exercise 29, write a reaction paragraph about the story. State your opinions about the family's situation. Use these questions to guide you: Is the family successful or unsuccessful? What is their main problem? How does the problem affect the family members? Is there a solution to their problem? Explain.

Focusing on Women's Studies: Key Women's Issues

EXERCISE 31   **Transferring reading ideas to your experience**

Discuss the following questions with your study group. Then, write your answers in complete sentences on separate paper.

1. In Selection 3, Martin is the father in the family, but he, rather than his wife, seems to be the chief caregiver for the children. Do you know any father in a similar situation? What is the reason for him being the main person to care for his children? Explain.
2. The main problem the family faces is Emily's alcoholism. Do you know someone who has a drinking problem? Does this problem affect her or his relationships within the family? If so, in what ways?
3. Another important element in the story is the children. How would you describe the mother-children relationship? Do you know of a family with a similar relationship between the mother and children? If so, describe the family.
4. The title of this story is "A Domestic Dilemma." The word *dilemma* suggests that Martin has a choice to make. What do you think his choice or choices are? Do you know of a couple who face a serious *dilemma*? If so, describe the couple's dilemma.

▷ Reading Journal

Write a one-page journal entry to expand your answer to one of the questions in Exercise 31. Use information from "A Domestic Dilemma" and from your own experience and knowledge to support your ideas.

◢ Linking Concepts

EXERCISE 32 **Synthesizing ideas from readings**

The women writers in this chapter present differing opinions and situations regarding male-female relationships and family duties. In the chart below are five topics. Think about how the writers of "Lessons for Women" and "A Domestic Dilemma" characterize each topic in their writing. Find a sentence from each reading that shows how the writer presents the topic. Write down the paragraph number in which you found the sentence. One answer is provided below as an example. Write your answers on separate paper. Be prepared to explain your ideas to your study group members.

Topic 1: A husband's control of his wife	Selection 1 Sentence Let her endure when others speak or do evil to her. (¶1)
	Selection 3 Sentence
Topic 2: A woman's language	Selection 1 Sentence
	Selection 3 Sentence
Topic 3: A woman's reaction when someone speaks badly to her	Selection 1 Sentence
	Selection 3 Sentence
Topic 4: A woman's work at home	Selection 1 Sentence
	Selection 3 Sentence
Topic 5: A woman's denial of her bad actions	Selection 1 Sentence
	Selection 3 Sentence

In your study group, compare your notes in the box above. Then, discuss the five topics as they relate to the ideas in Selection 2, "At Last Free." Does the writer of Selection 2 write about all five topics in her poem? If not all five, which topics does she mention? Share your answers with the class.

▷ Learning Vocabulary

EXERCISE 33 Studying synonyms

Find a synonym in Selection 3 for each underlined word in the sentences below. Write the synonyms on the lines. Check your answers with a classmate.

1. ... during the cold, <u>unproductive</u> months the yard was <u>bare</u> and the cottage seemed naked.

   unproductive = _____

   bare = _____

2. The children <u>shouted</u> a <u>surprising</u> welcome.

   shouted = _____

   surprising = _____

3. She <u>moved quickly</u> towards him and her kiss smelled like sherry. When he stood unresponsive she moved back a <u>step</u> and <u>laughed</u> nervously.

   moved quickly = _____

   step = _____

   laughed = _____

4. The revelations of <u>lack of control</u> <u>harmfully</u> <u>threatened</u> his previous <u>opinions</u> about his wife.

   lack of control = _____

   harmfully = _____

   threatened = _____

   opinions = _____

5. There were times of unexplainable <u>hatred</u>, times when the alcoholic fuse caused an explosion of <u>improper</u> anger.

   hatred = _____

   improper = _____

EXERCISE 34 **Reviewing academic vocabulary**

Study the academic words in the box.

accommodate	acknowledge	adjacent	alternative
anticipate	complexity	encounter	expose
inconsistent	infinitely	insufficient	restrain
restrain	revelation	scheme	trace, v.
unresponsive			

Then, discuss the following questions with your study group. Take notes on your discussion. Write answers to each question on separate paper. Copy down the questions, and write your answers in complete sentences.

1. When a hotel clerk says that he will **accommodate** all your needs, what is he saying?
2. How do you **acknowledge** your instructor when he or she walks past you in the hallway?
3. What is **adjacent** to the room in which you have your English class?
4. Do you have an **alternative** way to travel besides the usual way you travel?
5. What is the next special event that you **anticipate**?
6. Name one **complexity** in your life.
7. What do you do when you **encounter** an unfamiliar word in your reading?
8. What can happen when people **expose** their uncovered bodies to sunlight?
9. Do you have a skill in which your performance is **inconsistent**? Describe your performance.
10. If a mother is **infinitely** proud of her children, just how proud is she?
11. What do you do if you have **insufficient** time to finish a test?
12. How many generations back can you **trace** your family?
13. If you pick up the telephone and it is **unresponsive**, what happens?

EXERCISE 35 Reviewing academic vocabulary

Put a check mark next to the academic vocabulary words from Selection 3 that you already know.

accommodate	acknowledged	adjacent	adult
affected	alternative	analyze	anticipate
areas	complexity	couple	encounter
expose	featured	finally	images
inconsistent	infinitely	insufficient	nevertheless
restrain	revelations	schemes	secure
sought	source	tension	terminal
trace, *v.*	transferred	unresponsive	vision

Add unfamiliar words to your academic vocabulary list. For each unfamiliar word, write the word and its definition, and write a sentence using the word.

Example:

insufficient = not sufficient, inadequate

I have an insufficient amount of money to buy a new car, so I'm looking for a used car.

◺ Assessing Your Learning at the End of a Chapter

Revisiting Objectives

Return to the first page of this chapter. Think about the chapter objectives. Put a check mark in the box next to the ones you feel secure about. Review material in the chapter you still need to work on. When you are ready, answer the chapter review questions below.

▽ Practicing for a Chapter Test

EXERCISE 36 **Reviewing comprehension**

Check your comprehension of main concepts, or ideas, in this chapter by answering the following questions. First, write notes to answer the questions without looking back at the readings. Then, use the readings to check your answers and revise them, if necessary. Write your final answers in complete sentences on separate paper.

1. According to Selection 1, "Lessons for Women," what are the four important rules of behavior for women?

2. In written arguments, the writer usually organizes her or his ideas by first stating a _____ and then giving _____.

3. In Selection 2, "At Last Free," how did the writer describe her late husband's feelings towards her?

4. List one activity in the Selection 2 writer's former married life that she did not like.

5. In Selection 3, "A Domestic Dilemma," choose one of the descriptors below that best characterizes the level of success in Martin and Emily's relationship.
   a. very successful
   b. very unsuccessful
   c. somewhat unsuccessful

6. Write one sentence to state one of the problems that Emily has in the story "A Domestic Dilemma."

7. Write one sentence to state one of the worries that Martin has in the story "A Domestic Dilemma."

EXERCISE 37 Reviewing academic vocabulary

Check your knowledge of the academic words in this chapter. Read the sentence in which each word is used, and then circle a synonym for the word. The part of speech (noun, verb, adjective, adverb) is given. Compare your answers in your study group. Study the words you do not know.

1. deny, *v.*   Don't try to deny that you committed the crime.

accept	dispute	agree	confirm

2. conduct, *n.*   Michael learned to display good conduct in his first-grade class.

rules	mistakes	motive	behavior

3. authority, *n.*   Who should have the final authority in a family?

employee	obedience	power	inferiority

4. abandon, *v.*   If you abandon your goals, you'll never reach them.

defend	leave	indicate	endure

5. exhibit, *v.*   The museum will exhibit paintings from Southeast Asia.

show	continue	cover	hide

6. analyze, *v.*   You must analyze your problem and try to solve it.

investigate	neglect	use	believe in

7. restrain, *v.*   It's sometimes difficult to restrain your feelings.

express	show	control	hide

8. revelation, *n.*   A strange revelation about her past became known to us.

system	celebration	separation	discovery

9. scheme, *n.*   The criminal had a good scheme for robbing the bank.

plan	prevention	reason	tool

10. tension, *n.*   John felt the tension build as he walked into his boss's office.

power	peacefulness	stress	temperature

Extensive Reading

Work with a partner or on your own to find a piece of literature written by a woman or about women. Write a summary and reaction paragraph about the writing. Choose one interesting paragraph or page from the book. Photocopy the text. On your copy, write the name of the book and the author. Then, read the entire paragraph or page. Follow the instructions in the margin in writing a summary and reaction paragraph about the reading.

Possible Sources for Literature

Specific women authors

Go to a library to find literature written by the women authors whose books and stories were discussed at the beginning of this chapter: *Frankenstein* (Mary Wollstonecraft Shelley), *Little Women* (Louisa May Alcott), *The Joy Luck Club* (Amy Tan), *Harry Potter* (J. K. Rowling), *Pride and Prejudice* (Jane Austen), *Bridget Jones' Diary* (Helen Fielding), and "The Birds" (Daphne du Maurier). You can search the library's online catalog or ask a librarian to help you.

Women writers

Go to a library and ask a librarian to help you find literature written by women authors. Or use the Internet to identify women authors. Do a search by typing in the words "women writers." Follow the guidelines at elt.heinle.com/collegereading for using the Internet. Then, go to a library to locate specific books.

Women in literature

Go to a library and ask a librarian to help you find literature about women. Or use the Internet to identify women in literature. Do a search by typing in the words "women literature." Follow the guidelines at elt.heinle.com/collegereading for using the Internet. Then, go to a library to locate specific books.

Master Student Tip

▼ Reaction Paragraph

Find one or two sentences from the reading that contain an interesting or important idea. Copy the sentence on a sheet of paper. First, write a sentence or sentences to summarize the ideas in the sentence. Then, state your opinion about this idea. Do you agree with it? Do you have experience that shows the idea is true? Explain by citing your own experience or the experience of others.

WEB POWER

Go to **elt.heinle.com/collegereading** to view more readings on literature and women's studies, plus exercises that will help you study the Web readings and the academic words in this chapter.

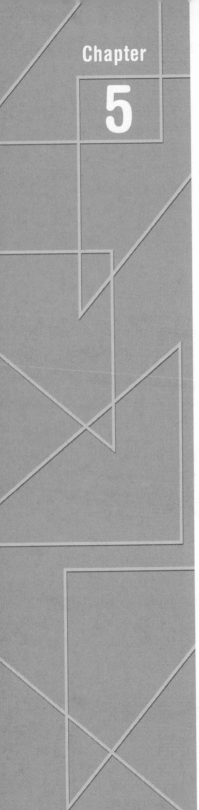

Cracking the Ice Age

ACADEMIC FOCUS: GEOLOGY AND ARCHAEOLOGY

Portage Glacier near Anchorage, Alaska

Academic Reading Objectives

After completing this chapter,
you should be able to:

✓ Check here as you
master each objective.

1. Know more vocabulary words used in
   your academic studies ☐
2. Create graphic organizers to help you
   see and remember important ideas in reading ☐
3. Recognize and understand the language of
   certain and uncertain ideas in reading ☐
4. Know the meanings of common word roots ☐

Geology and Archaeology Objectives

1. Understand general information about
   geology and archaeology ☐
2. Expand your knowledge by viewing and
   writing about an educational film ☐

Reading Assignment 1

THE STORY BEHIND THE ICE AGE

▷ Getting Ready to Read

Focusing on Geology and Archaeology

EXERCISE 1 Participating in class discussion

Discuss the following questions with your classmates.

1. Read the definition of *geology*.

   ge•ol•o•gy *n.*   the science that studies the origin, history, and structure of the earth

   What questions do *geologists* try to answer?

2. Read the definition of *archaeology*.

   ar•chae•ol•o•gy *n.*   the scientific recovery and study of the remains of past human activities, such as burials, buildings, and tools

   How is *geology* different from *archaeology*?

3. The photograph at the beginning of this chapter depicts a large *glacier* in Alaska. What do you think of when you look at this photograph? Imagine you were a geologist or an archaeologist. What would you think about when you looked at the photograph?

EXERCISE 2 Reading titles and previewing information

Read the titles of the reading selections below. Think about the selections you will read.

Selections

1. "The Story behind the Ice Age"
2. "The Iceman Cometh"
3. "Kill, Chill, or Ill? What Happened to Ice Age Mammals?"

Discuss the following questions with your study group. Take notes on what your group members know. This will help prepare you to read.

1. Selection 1 describes the most recent *ice age.* Write down three general things you know about the Ice Age.

   a. _____

   b. _____

   c. _____

2. Selection 1 also discusses Earth's current climate and the possibilities of another ice age. Do scientists think Earth is getting colder or getting warmer?

   _____

   _____

3. Selection 2 tells the story of humans during the Ice Age. What do you know (or what can you imagine) about people who lived in the Ice Age? What might they have worn? How might they have slept? What did they probably eat?

   _____

   _____

4. Archaeologists continue to look for evidence of human travels during the Ice Age. What do you know (or what can you guess) about how humans traveled during the Ice Age? Where might they have traveled? Why would they have traveled?

   _____

   _____

5. From the title of Selection 3, what can you guess are three popular theories about what happened to large Ice Age animals?

   _____

   _____

6. Finally, Selection 3 describes Ice Age *mammals* that no longer exist. What are *mammals?* Which Ice Age mammals do you know about?

   _____

   _____

◤ Reading for a Purpose

EXERCISE 3 **Predicting content before reading**

As you learned in Chapter 3, predicting content before you read helps you prepare for reading. Test your knowledge of the Ice Age. Mark the following statements T for true or F for false. Compare your answers in your study group.

1. _____ The most recent ice age started about one billion years ago.

2. _____ In this ice age, ice covered all of Russia.

3. _____ Ice sheets move forward and back over land during an ice age.

4. _____ Currently, Earth is in a warming period.

5. _____ Scientists are not certain what caused the last ice age.

6. _____ There is no evidence that other ice ages occurred in Earth's history.

7. _____ Some scientists think that changes in Earth's motion could cause an ice age.

◤ Reading for Information

As you have done in previous chapters, read Selection 1 the first time without consulting a dictionary. Then, reread it as many times as necessary, using a dictionary to look up unfamiliar words. As you read, highlight or underline important ideas in the text. Here's an example of how you might annotate a section of this reading:

Ice sheets covered Canada, No. Amer. & Europe

About one million years ago it was as cold in much of northern North America and northern Europe as it is today in Greenland. Great ice sheets developed over central and eastern Canada and northern Scandinavia. In North America the ice sheets developed over an area that extends as far south as where the Ohio and Mississippi rivers meet and eastward to central Long Island. Much of the north central and northeastern parts of the United States were covered by ice. In Europe the ice sheets covered most of Scandinavia, the British Isles, Denmark, Belgium, northern France, and the Baltic countries and reached far into Germany and Russia.

Ice sheets covered North America during the last ice age.

Reading Selection 1

"THE STORY BEHIND THE ICE AGE"

1   About one million years ago it was as cold in much of northern North America and northern Europe as it is today in Greenland. Great ice sheets developed over central and eastern Canada and northern Scandinavia. In North America the ice sheets developed over an area that extends[1] as far south as where the Ohio and Mississippi rivers meet and eastward to central Long Island. Much of the north central and northeastern parts of the United States were covered by ice. In Europe the ice sheets covered most of Scandinavia, the British Isles, Denmark, Belgium, northern France, and the Baltic countries and reached far into Germany and Russia.

---

1. *extends* = reaches, goes as far as

2   The ice sheets advanced and receded[2] four major times during the million-year period as the climate changed from cold to warm and back again. The last time the ice sheets receded was about 11,000 years ago. Many geologists think we are now in a warm, or *interglacial*, period that will be followed by a return of the ice sheets in perhaps 20,000 years. Others think that this warm period will last millions of years.

3   To explain why Earth was cold enough to have the recent Ice Age, certain facts must be considered:

1. This Ice Age began about 1 million years ago and included four major advances of the ice sheets.
2. Warm interglacial periods came after each advance. Earth may now be in an interglacial period.
3. Other ice ages have occurred from time to time in the past 600 million years.
4. During the last Ice Age, glaciers advanced and receded at the same time in both the Northern and Southern hemispheres.

4   Geologists have proposed many hypotheses to account for[3] ice ages. One idea is that the amount of heat energy given off by the sun changes. Ice ages may occur during periods when energy from the sun is less. Or the amount of energy reaching Earth might change due to volcanic dust in the atmosphere. Another possibility is that during periods of mountain building, more of Earth's land area lay above the snow line.[4] More land under snow might change the climate enough for an ice age to begin. A fourth idea concerns the former position of continents on Earth's surface. If continents used to be in the way of currents[5] between oceans, they may have prevented the mixing of cold and warm water. Without mixing between oceans, areas of Earth might become cold enough to start an ice age. Each of these hypotheses has its strong and weak points. Recent research has added to knowledge about the times and durations[6] of the previous Ice Age. Geologists have also discovered evidence of many more ice ages in the distant past.

2. *receded* = moved back from a limit or point
3. *to account for* = to explain or give the reason for something
4. *snow line* = the lowest level that permanent snow reaches in summer
5. *currents* = continuous movements of water in a particular direction
6. *durations* = periods of time during which something lasts

5   A hypothesis that explains much of the new evidence being found concerns changes in the motions of Earth itself. Changes in the tilt[7] of Earth's axis[8] and in the shape of its orbit[9] might cause colder climates on some parts of Earth. Changes of this kind do take place over and over again at regular intervals[10] in Earth's history, which might explain why ice ages happen periodically. Also, such changes in Earth's position could cause glacial climates in both hemispheres[11] at the same time. Did the Ice Age occur because of changes in Earth's position and motion? Scientists must study all new evidence to see whether it supports the hypothesis, or to determine whether the hypothesis must be modified.

Source: D.C. Heath. (1999). *Earth Science.* Evanston, IL: D.C. Heath (a division of Houghton Mifflin Co.).

▷ Assessing Your Learning

Demonstrating Comprehension

EXERCISE 4   **Expressing the main idea**

Write one sentence to express the main idea of the reading. Include both

   a. *the general topic of the reading and*
   b. *the main points the writer tells us about the topic.*

Compare your sentence with a partner's, and then discuss your answer with the class.

7. *tilt* = a slant; a position in which one side is higher than the other
8. *Earth's axis* = an imaginary straight line through Earth, around which Earth rotates
9. *orbit* = the path traveled by an object that is moving around a larger object
10. *intervals* = amounts of time between two events
11. *hemisphere* = one half Earth, especially the northern or southern parts above and below the equator

EXERCISE 5   Checking your self-test

Work with a partner to check the answers to the True/False questions you answered before reading. Next to each statement, write the paragraph number in which the idea is stated. Rewrite false statements to make them true. Compare your answers in your study group.

Study the examples of graphic organizers:

EXERCISE 6   Creating graphic organizers

Study the examples of graphic organizers.

1. Cluster Map shows qualities or characteristics of a main idea.

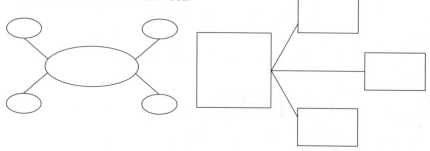

2. Central Idea Organizer shows a main idea and supporting details.

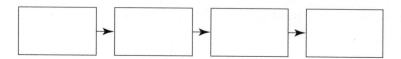

3. Flow chart shows a series of events.

Next, create two graphic organizers to show important ideas in Selection 1. Share and explain your graphic organizers with your study group. Follow the directions below.

First, make a cluster map. In the center circle, write "Recent Ice Age." Then, in smaller circles connected by lines to the center circle, write facts and details that scientists know about the recent ice age. Include dates and place names. Do not write complete sentences. Write the facts and details in words or phrases. Use abbreviations. The example cluster map has been partially completed to give you an idea of how to start your map.

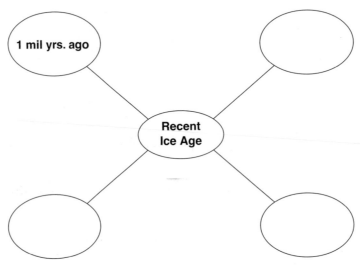

Example Cluster Map

Second, create a flow chart such as the one on the next page. In the first box, write "Recent Ice Age began: 1 mil yrs ago." In the next boxes, briefly write the important events that happened in the Ice Age in the order of time. Include dates and place names. Your last box should contain facts and details about the period we are in now. (You used a flow chart in Chapter 2, "What Makes You You?" This flow chart showed the steps in the scientific method.)

Here's an example of how you might start your flow chart:

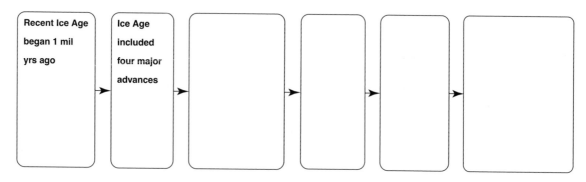

Example Flow Chart

Discuss this question in your group: Which of the two organizers better presents the important ideas about the recent ice age? Why?

▷ Linking Concepts

EXERCISE 7   **Applying the scientific method**

In Chapter 2, you studied the scientific method of research. Look back at the flow chart on page 54 that shows the steps in the scientific method. With a partner, discuss the steps of the scientific method that scientists use to study the Ice Age.

1. With your partner, begin a flow chart to present the scientific steps that have been used to study hypotheses relating to the <u>cause</u> of the Ice Age. Copy the flow chart printed below on a sheet of paper. Include the general "labels" included in each box. In the "Ask a question" box, write the question that scientists are trying to answer.
2. In the "Form a hypothesis" box, you and your partner will write one sentence to express <u>one</u> of the five hypotheses that scientists have made about the cause of the Ice Age. Your instructor may assign you one hypothesis to work on. Look back at Selection 1 to find the hypotheses. Write your hypothesis in simple words with abbreviations.

The Scientific Method

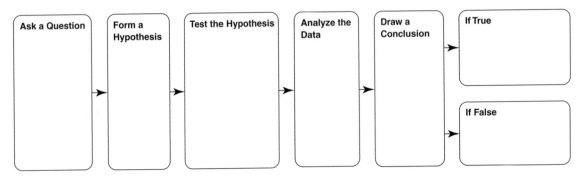

Ask a Question	Form a Hypothesis	Test the Hypothesis	Analyze the Data	Draw a Conclusion	If True

If False

3. Show your flow chart to your study group. Next, gather ideas about the next step—how scientists might test their hypotheses. In the "Test the hypothesis" box, write your ideas about things scientists might study to prove the hypothesis is true. In other words, briefly write possible methods that scientists could use to test the hypothesis. What kinds of tests could they conduct? Use the scientific method chart on page 54 as a resource for what to write here.

4. For the "Analyze the data" box, write down ideas about how scientists might decide if the information they got from their tests was accurate. If you don't have any ideas, copy the information from the "Analyze the data" box on page 54.

5. Next, discuss whether scientists have reached a conclusion about whether the hypothesis has been proved as the cause for the Ice Age. In the "Draw a conclusion" box, write a phrase to state whether the hypothesis has been proved true or false. Use the information from Selection 1, "The Story behind the Ice Age," to help you fill in this box.

6. Present and explain your flow charts to the class.

◩ Reading Journal

Write a one-page entry about the hypothesis you think best explains the cause of the Ice Age. Use information from the reading. Use logical explanations to defend your idea that one hypothesis is more likely to explain the true cause for the Ice Age.

▷ Learning Vocabulary

EXERCISE 8   Reviewing academic vocabulary

Read the list of nine academic words in the right-hand column below. From the sentences on the left, choose the sentence that best defines each word. Compare your answers with a partner's.

1. Facts, objects, or signs that make you believe that something exists or is true are called _____.	area
	occurred
2. When something happens again and again, usually at regular times, we say that it happens _____.	hypothesis
	energy
3. Serious study of a subject that is intended to discover new facts about it is known as _____.	research
	evidence
4. An idea that is suggested as an explanation of something but that has not yet been proved to be true is called a _____.	intervals
	periodically
5. When you make small changes to something in order to improve it, the thing is _____.	modified
6. Periods of time between two events or activities are called _____.	

EXERCISE 9   Reviewing academic vocabulary

Put a check mark next to the academic vocabulary words from Selection 1 that you already know.

area	hypothesis(es)	research	evidence
major	occur(red)	previous	intervals
periodically	modified		

Add unfamiliar words to your academic vocabulary list. For each unfamiliar word, write the word and its definition, and write a sentence using the word.

Reading Assignment 2

THE ICEMAN COMETH

▷ Getting Ready to Read

EXERCISE 10 Guessing unfamiliar words in reading

Before you read Selection 2, "The Iceman Cometh," study the sentences in the chart below. Guess the meaning of each bold-faced word <u>without</u> using a dictionary. Use other words in the sentences to help you guess the meaning of the words. Pay attention to the part of speech and the positive/negative meaning of each word. Check the definition on the right that makes the most sense.

1. **Herds** of wild animals from Siberia, including the **mastodon**, migrated across the flat, treeless plains of the Beringia land bridge.	**herds** ____ groups ____ parts	**mastodon** ____ a type of animal ____ a type of tree
2. Elephant-eating **jaguars** stand tall as lions.	**jaguar** ____ a kind of wild cat ____ a kind of bear	
3. With arctic cold pushing so far southward, **walrus bask** on Virginia beaches …	**walrus** ____ land animal ____ sea animal	**bask** ____ lie ____ swim ____ run

Compare your answers with a partner's. Then, check your answers in a dictionary.

▷ Reading for a Purpose

Reading for Information

As you did with Selection 1, read Selection 2, "The Iceman Cometh," once without stopping. Do not use a dictionary. Then, reread the text as many times as necessary. Look up unfamiliar words. Write their definitions in the margins of the reading. Mark the main idea and major points of the reading with underlining, highlighting, and margin notes.

A drawing of an Ice Age man in Great Britain

Reading Selection 2

"THE ICEMAN COMETH"

1   During the last Ice Age, the buildup of glaciers locked up huge amounts of Earth's waters. As a result, sea levels were lower, allowing for people to migrate across the ice sheets in several parts of the world.

2   In America, the Ice Age created a land corridor[1] between Asia and Alaska across what is now the Bering Strait.[2] The first inhabitants arrived sometime toward the end of this Ice Age.

1. *corridor* = an open area of land forming a passageway between two larger areas
2. *Bering Strait* = the narrow passage of water that joins Asia and Alaska

3   Herds of wild animals from Siberia, including the mastodon, migrated across the flat, treeless plains of the Beringia land bridge. Gradually, Siberian hunters followed these animals into North America. They most likely were unaware that they were entering a new continent.[3] These migrants[4] were the ancestors of the native Americans of North and South America.

4   Thomas Canby, a writer for *National Geographic* magazine, spent a year with archaeologists as they searched for ancient burial sites throughout the Americas. From his experience, Canby envisioned[5] the type of world that might have greeted the first Americans:

> What a wild world it was! To see it properly, we must board[6] a time machine and travel back into the Ice Age. The northern half of North America has vanished,[7] buried beneath ice sheets two miles thick. Stretching south to Kentucky, they buckle[8] the Earth's crust with their weight . . .. Animals grow oversize . . .. Elephant-eating jaguars stand tall as lions, beavers grow as big as bears, South American sloths as tall as giraffes. With arctic cold pushing so far southward, walrus bask on Virginia beaches, and musk-oxen graze[9] from Maryland to California.

5   No one knows for sure when the first Americans arrived. Some scholars contend that the migration across the land bridge began as early as 40,000 BC. Others argue it occurred as late as 12,000 BC.

6   Archaeologists have also found evidence that suggests that early humans crossed land bridges in many other parts of the world. The first humans in Ireland may have crossed a land bridge to England in 7,000 BC, and between England and France in 16,000 BC. Land bridges may also have connected southern Europe with North Africa. In the Pacific Ocean, New Guinea and Australia were thought to have been joined by a land bridge until about 8,000 BC.

Source: Adapted from McDougal Littell (2001). *World History: Patterns of Interaction.*

---

3. *continent* = one of the seven great land areas of Earth
4. *migrants* = people who migrate, or regularly move from one area or country to another
5. *envisioned* = pictured in the mind; imagined something as a future possibility
6. *board* = to get on or in a vehicle
7. *vanished* = disappeared
8. *buckle* = to bend because of heat or pressure, or to make something do this
9. *graze* = to feed on grass

▷ Assessing Your Learning

Demonstrating Comprehension

EXERCISE 11 **Expressing the main idea**

Which of the following sentences best expresses the writer's main idea? Check the best main idea sentence. Compare your answer with a classmate's. Then, discuss the answer with the class.

_____ In the Ice Age, men traveled on ice sheets and hunted animals.

_____ A land bridge connected Asia and Alaska during the Ice Age.

_____ Oversized animals lived during the Ice Age.

_____ This reading is about people who lived during the Ice Age.

POWER GRAMMAR

Recognizing Words That Signal Possibility

Academic readings, especially science readings, often use two very different kinds of sentences:

1. Some sentences state certainties. The writer is sure the information is accurate.
2. Other sentences give hypotheses, theories, and other "educated guesses." The writer is not so sure this kind of information is completely accurate.

Being able to recognize when a writer is claiming accuracy or being tentative (not certain) is an important skill for an academic reader. Compare these sentences from Selection 2:

1. During the last Ice Age, glaciers advanced and receded at the same time in both the Northern and Southern hemispheres.
2. The first humans in Ireland may have crossed a land bridge to England in 7,000 BC.

Sentence 1 states a *certainty*. Notice that the writer uses the *simple past tense* verb to state the idea. However, sentence 2 contains the verb *may have crossed*. The use of the modal auxiliary verb *may* (which can mean "possibility") tells the reader that the writer is *uncertain* about the accuracy of this information.

(Continued)

A writer may claim certainty or accuracy by using these language features:

▶ Simple present tense verbs, when the fact is still true

Example Earth is round.

▶ Past tense verbs, when the fact is about something that occurred in the past

Example The most recent Ice Age began about one million years ago.

▶ Present perfect verbs, to refer to a period of time in the past that started in the past and continues until now

Example Other ice ages have occurred from time to time in the past 600 million years.

In contrast, a writer may indicate uncertainty by using these features:

▶ Modal auxiliary verbs of possibility: *can, may, might, could*

Example Ice ages may occur during periods when energy from the sun is less.

▶ Verbs that indicate uncertainty like *think, believe, contend, argue, suggest, propose, be thought to be, guess,* etc.

Example Many geologists think we are now in a warm, or interglacial, period.

▶ Other words that indicate unproven ideas, like *possible/possibly/possibility, probable/probability/probably, likely/likelihood, theory/theorize, hypothesis, suggestion, perhaps, maybe,* etc.

Example Another possibility is that during periods of mountain building, more of Earth's land area lay above the snow line.

EXERCISE 12 **Recognizing certain and uncertain ideas**

Read these sentences taken from Selections 1 and 2. Mark the sentences containing certain *ideas "C," and the sentences containing* uncertain *ideas, "U." Underline the language in each of the sentences that helped you recognize the type of sentence. Compare your answers in your study group.*

1. _____ During the last Ice Age, the buildup of glaciers locked up huge amounts of the Earth's waters. (Selection 1, ¶ 3)

2. _____ Also, such changes in Earth's position could cause glacial climates in both hemispheres at the same time. (Selection 1, ¶ 5)

3. _____ In America, the Ice Age created a land corridor between Asia and Alaska across what is now the Bering Strait. (Selection 2, ¶ 2)

4. _____ They [hunters] most likely were unaware that they were entering a new continent. (Selection 2, ¶ 3)

5. _____ These migrants were the ancestors of the native Americans of North and South America. (Selection 2, ¶ 3)

6. _____ Some scholars contend that the migration across the land bridge began as early as 40,000 BC. Others argue it occurred as late as 12,000 BC. (Selection 2, ¶ 5)

7. _____ In the Pacific Ocean, New Guinea and Australia were thought to have been joined by a land bridge until about 8,000 BC. (Selection 2, ¶ 6)

EXERCISE 13 **Expressing certain and uncertain ideas**

Academic readers should be careful to notice the language that writers use to express certainty *and* uncertainty. *Sometimes writers claim certainty when they shouldn't, so we have to be especially careful readers. Evaluate the following sentences. Which ones seem to be claiming too much certainty and should be revised to be less certain? Rewrite the sentences as necessary. Compare your answers with a partner's.*

1. Grains found in the body of an iceman in the Alps prove that he had eaten eight hours before he died.

2. All ice age men ate grains.

3. The Alps iceman was carrying early tools: a bow and an arrow.

4. Unfortunately, the officials who removed the iceman damaged his bones.

5. Scientists damage human remains and objects when they remove them from a site.

6. An ice age hunter always traveled alone when hunting animals.

7. The most recent ice age was caused by changes in Earth's motion.

▷ Questions for Discussion

EXERCISE 14 **Participating in group discussion**

Discuss the following questions in your study group. Then, write answers to the questions in complete sentences on separate paper.

1. From the information in Selections 1 and 2, what do you think early humans needed to do to survive?
2. Look at these photographs of early tools. For what purposes do you think early humans used their tools? What modern tools does each of these early tools resemble?

Ancient arrowheads made of wood

A stone blade

Harpoons for fishing, made from an animal horn

▷ Learning Vocabulary

EXERCISE 15 **Working with word families**

*In Chapters 2 and 3, you studied word families and word endings. Read the
list of words in the left-hand column of the box. Write the paragraph
number in which each word appears. Find each word in Selection 2, and
write its part of speech (n. for noun, v. for verb, adj. for adjective, adv. for
adverb). Then, add other members of the word family and their parts of
speech in the right-hand columns. Use a dictionary to help you. The first
one is done as an example. Compare your answers with a partner's.*

Selection 2 words	Paragraph	Part of speech	Other words in "family"	Part of speech
migrate	1, 3 (-ed)	v.	migrational	adj.
migrants	3	n.	migrator	n.
migration	5	n.	migratory	adj.
inhabitants				
inhabited				
created				
creation				
archaeologists				
archaeology				
burial				
buried				

*Next, complete the words in the sentences. Use words from the chart above.
You may have to add additional endings to verbs.*

EARLY HUMAN DISCOVERIES

Archaeolog_____ continue to learn more about early humans who inhabit_____ Earth during the most recent ice age. Scientists have learned this by studying the remains of Ice Age inhabit_____. One iceman was bur_____ in the Alps until he was discovered in 1991 by hikers. Other ancient people have been found throughout Europe. Mountains and wetlands have proved to be perfect bur_____ sites because the climate and land have creat_____ good environments for keeping human remains in good condition. Some Ice Age people inhabit_____ caves, where archaeolog_____ have found the remains of bodies. They have also discovered household objects bur_____ in cave homes. Another subject of inquiry in the field of archaeolog_____ is the migra_____ of humans from one area to another. During the Ice Age, it is believed that humans migra_____ from one continent to another. Objects that have been found by scientists show that these early migra_____ carried arts and crafts from Asia to the Americas. Scientists have creat_____ "virtual" maps on the computer to show the migra_____ patterns of early humans. The field of archaeolog_____ continues to shed more light on the Earth's early human inhabit_____.

EXERCISE 16 Studying words that are often used together

Words are often used in combination with other words. Read the sentences below, paying attention to the bold-faced words. Are these word combinations common? Circle the bold-faced word combinations that seem correct. Discuss your answers with your classmates. The first one is done for you.

1. I have a **major problem**.

   Ricky has a **major girlfriend**.

   Suzanne is my **major sister**. She's two years older than I.

   Kiev is the **major commercial center** in the Ukraine.

2. The **weather extended** over the weekend.

   The couple **extended a welcome** to their guests.

   He **extended his legs** and lay down on the couch.

3. Nora needs to **modify her diet**.

   We **modified our plans** because of the rain.

   Rena **modified her height** by wearing high-heeled shoes.

4. **Birds migrate** to the south in winter.

   Many **cars migrate** into the parking garage every evening.

   Farm workers migrate to different areas to harvest crops.

5. There's a lot of noise at the **construction site**.

   His **bedroom** is a peaceful **site**.

   Every year a reenactment is held at the **battlefield site**.

6. Researchers have **found evidence**.

   Mr. Jones **gave evidence** at the trial.

   Scientists need to **test evidence** carefully.

   The police **have evidence** that the murder took place at 10:00 p.m.

7. The undertaker **buried the body** in the cemetery.

   The young woman **buried her feelings** about her problems.

   The man's **glasses were buried** under a pile of papers.

Reading Assignment 3

KILL, CHILL, OR ILL? WHAT HAPPENED TO ICE AGE MAMMALS?

▷ Getting Ready to Read

EXERCISE 17 **Previewing the reading**

Read the title and examine the photographs before you read. Discuss these questions with your study group.

1. What do you expect Selection 3 to report about ice age mammals?
2. The reading presents possible causes for what happened to these large animals. What part do you think humans may have played? What part did climate possibly play?
3. What do you think scientists might look for today to discover what happened to the ice age mammals?

EXERCISE 18 **Predicting content before reading**

Test your knowledge of Ice Age mammals. Mark the following statements T for true or F for false. Compare your answers in your study group.

1. _____ More than 100 species of large mammals were wiped out during the Ice Age.

2. _____ Most scientists agree on the causes for the extinction (disappearance) of Ice Age mammals.

3. _____ Early human hunters may have killed all the Ice Age mammals.

4. _____ Ice Age mammals probably moved from place to place, as early humans did.

5. _____ Ice Age mammals might have carried diseases from one species to another.

6. _____ It's likely that cold weather killed some species of Ice Age mammals.

EXERCISE 19 Guessing unfamiliar words when reading

Before you read Selection 3, study the sentences in the left column of the box. Guess the meanings of the bold-faced words, using the context clues. Put a check mark next to the definition on the right that makes the most sense. Do not consult a dictionary.

1. Dr. Paul Martin, professor of geosciences at the University of Arizona's Desert Laboratory, says human hunters **dramatically** changed the landscape of North America in the past 13,000 years, wiping out some 40 species of large mammals	**dramatically** _____ suddenly and greatly _____ slowly and unnoticeably
2. When prey is easy to kill, large **predators** (wolves, spotted hyenas) may kill far more than they can consume.	**predators** _____ animals that are killed and eaten by other animals _____ animals that kill and eat other animals
3. From evidence it is clear that humans are not **assiduous** enough killers to take out every last animal in an area.	**assiduous** _____ evil _____ hardworking _____ careless
4. As humans gradually developed hunting skills, big animals could adjust to people's increasing **lethality** by changing their behavior	**lethality** _____ deadliness _____ harmlessness _____ helpfulness

Compare your answers with a partner's. Then, use a dictionary to check your work.

▷ Reading for Information

Read Selection 3, "Kill, Chill, or Ill? What Happened to Ice Age Mammals?" once without a dictionary. Then, reread it as many times as necessary with a dictionary. Write definitions of unfamiliar words in the margins. Highlight or underline important ideas for later study.

Reading Selection 3

KILL, CHILL, OR ILL? WHAT HAPPENED TO ICE AGE MAMMALS?

1   The ongoing mystery about what killed off some of the largest modern mammals[1] centers on three theories: human hunting ("Kill"), climate change ("Chill"), and plague[2] ("Ill"). A fourth school of thought holds that many factors converged[3] to cause mass extinctions[4] during the last ice age.

Kill School

2   Dr. Paul Martin, professor of geosciences at the University of Arizona's Desert Laboratory, says human hunters dramatically changed the landscape of North America in the past 13,000 years, wiping out some 40 species of large mammals, including mammoths, mastodons, native camels, ground sloths, short-faced bears, and saber-tooth cats.

3   According to Dr. Martin, a small number of humans were able to kill large populations of the now-extinct Ice Age mammals. "When prey[5] is easy to kill, large predators (wolves, spotted hyenas) may kill far more than they can consume. It's not a pleasant thought, but perhaps early hunters also overkilled easy prey," Dr. Martin says.

Chill School

4   For more than twenty years, Dr. Kenneth B. Tankersley has explored underground caverns worldwide in search of evidence that climate changes caused the extinction of massive ice age

---

1. *mammals* = animals, including humans, that drink milk from their mother's breasts when they are young
2. *plague* = an attack of a disease that spreads easily and kills a large number of people
3. *converged* = came together
4. *extinctions* = the state of being *extinct*, or no longer existing
5. *prey* = an animal hunted for food by another animal

mammals. A member of the Department of Art and Archaeology at Augustana College in Sioux Falls, S.D., Tankersley is coauthor of the new book *In Search of Ice Age Americans*. His research suggests that Ice Age animals were killed off because they moved around when the temperature changed. Dr. Tankersley writes:

> More than 300 dates have been recently obtained from the remains of [large and small mammals] using accelerator mass spectrometry.[6] They not only demonstrate that more than 30 [large mammals] became extinct at the end of the Ice Age, but they also document major range shifts of individual species. This situation is the direct result of individual species response to climatic change. In other words, each species has its own unique response to change. With the rapid and profound[7] global warming, some animals were able to move, others became smaller, and some became extinct.

Baluchitherium

Ill School

5   The curator[8] of the Department of Mammalogy at the American Museum of Natural History in New York, Dr. Ross MacPhee maintains that many "mega-mammal" extinctions in the past 40,000 years may have been caused by diseases introduced by humans or animals that traveled with them. The evidence is not conclusive that disease killed off the animals, according to Dr. MacPhee. He bases his argument on later extinctions of animals that were believed to be caused by disease, such as that of the

6. *accelerator mass spectrometry* = the measurement of energy waves by using a scientific instrument
7. *profound* = far-reaching; having a strong influence or effect
8. *curator* = a person who is in charge of a museum, library, or zoo

golden toad of Central America during the mid-1990s and the native rodents of Christmas Island. MacPhee argues that humans were not expert enough hunters to completely kill off species of animals, so the animals must have suffered from disease:

> As to the level of mortality[9] required to kill off a species—it has to be huge. This is precisely why humans-as-the-cause makes no sense. From evidence it is clear that humans are not assiduous enough killers to take out every last animal in an area, basically because there is no good reason to do so. (Since it gets harder and harder to find the "last" members of a species, why bother if there are other choices available?) It is very easy to blame humans for every problem that the planet currently suffers from, but there is not enough evidence to convict. I vote for disease because it is the only potential mechanism[10] we know of that can cause enough loss in a period short enough to lead to extinction.

Woolly mammoth

Combination School

6   Dr. David Burney, associate professor in the Department of Biological Studies at Fordham University, is convinced that no cause can be pinpointed as the sole reason for the mega beast extinctions. He bases his hypothesis on research of extinctions in North America, Africa, Madagascar, Hawaii, and the West Indies. Dr. Burney argues that animals became extinct for different reasons, depending on the area of the world:

9. *mortality* = the number of deaths in a particular period of time
10. *mechanism* = a process or means to do or create something

Elephants, camels, and horses, for instance, were abundant and diverse in both the Old World and the New. The critical difference is that, in Africa and Eurasia, large animals co-evolved with humans. Our earliest ancestors of a few million years ago were no threat to big animals. As humans gradually developed hunting skills, big animals could adjust to people's increasing lethality[11] by changing their behavior and ecology to give humans a wider berth.[12] In North and South America, on the other hand, most scientists believe that the first people these big animals saw were already highly skilled hunters who migrated across the Bering Land Bridge from Asia with spear-throwers, dogs, and an advanced social structure. These New World animals had never seen a human before, and probably had no fear of this new, unlikely-looking predator. That made the human hunter's job much easier.

Platybelodon

7   Furthermore, Dr. Burney is not convinced that disease could have killed so many species. "A disease that kills all species quickly is unknown to science," he argues. Even so, he explains, disease could have killed some species, possibly carried by another species that became sick, but did not die, of the disease.

Source: Adapted from
http://dsc.discovery.com/convergence/megabeasts/experts/experts.html.

11. *lethality* = ability to kill some living thing
12. *to give someone/something a wider berth* = slang, to keep enough space or distance from someone/something to avoid an unwanted result

▽ Assessing Your Learning

Demonstrating Comprehension

EXERCISE 20 Expressing the main idea

Find one sentence from Selection 3 that expresses the main idea. Be sure the sentence includes both the topic of the reading and the writer's attitude, opinion, or idea about it. Compare your answer with your classmates'.

EXERCISE 21 Creating a graphic organizer

Study the graphic organizer below, which visually tells about one "school," or theory, that explains the extinction of Ice Age mammals. Work with a partner to answer these questions:

1. Does the organizer clearly show the central idea?
2. Does it include the most important points made in the reading about the "ill" school?
3. If not, add other boxes with additional points about this theory.

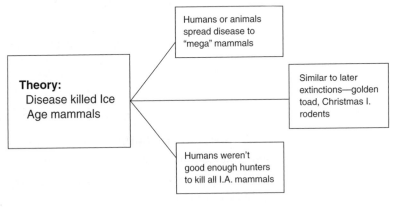

Theory:
Disease killed Ice Age mammals

Humans or animals spread disease to "mega" mammals

Similar to later extinctions—golden toad, Christmas I. rodents

Humans weren't good enough hunters to kill all I.A. mammals

The "Ill" School

Work with a partner to create three additional graphic organizers to represent the other theories about what killed Ice Age mammals. Choose one of the types of graphic organizers shown earlier in this chapter. The main idea in each of your organizers should be a phrase that identifies the theory. In your organizer, include the major points in the theory and any important supporting details. Share your graphic organizers in your study group.

EXERCISE 22 **Distinguishing between theories and support**

In Chapter 2, you learned that science readings are often organized into series of theories and support sentences. Read the sentences in the box. Check if the sentence expresses a theory or a supporting idea. Think about these two points as you read each sentence:

1. Look at the graphic organizers you just made in Exercise 20. Your organizers should show the difference between main ideas (theories) and support. You may have included some of the ideas in the "theory" and "support" sentences in your organizers.
2. Look for language that expresses the writer's *certainty* (because *facts* are one type of support) or *uncertainty*. The language features appear on pages 187–188. Sentences that express *uncertainty* are likely to be "theory" sentences. Sentences that express *certainty* are likely to be "support" (because *facts* are one type of support).

1. The ongoing mystery about what killed off some of the largest modern mammals centers on three theories: human hunting ("Kill"), climate change ("Chill"), and plague ("Ill"). (¶ 1)	___ Theory? ___ Support?
2. A fourth school of thought holds that many factors converged to cause mass extinctions during the last ice age. (¶ 1)	___ Theory? ___ Support?
3. "When prey is easy to kill, large predators (wolves, spotted hyenas) may kill far more than they can consume . . .," Dr. Martin says. (¶ 3)	___ Theory? ___ Support?
4. His [Tankersley's] research suggests that Ice Age animals were killed off because they moved around when the temperature changed. (¶ 4)	___ Theory? ___ Support?
5. More than 300 dates have been recently obtained from the remains of [large and small mammals] using accelerator mass spectrometry. (¶ 4)	___ Theory? ___ Support?

6. Dr. Burney argues that animals became extinct for different reasons, depending on the area of the world. (¶ 6)	_____ Theory? _____ Support?
7. In North and South America, on the other hand, most scientists believe that the first people these big animals saw were already highly skilled hunters . . . (¶ 6)	_____ Theory? _____ Support?

EXERCISE 23 **Checking your self-test**

Work with a partner to check the answers to the True/False questions you answered before reading. Next to each statement, write the paragraph number in which the idea is stated. Rewrite false statements to make them true. Compare your answers in your study group.

▷ Questions for Discussion

EXERCISE 24 **Participating in group discussion**

Discuss the following questions with your study group. Take notes on your discussion. Write your answers in complete sentences on separate paper.

1. Read the names of extinct mammals in paragraph 2 of Selection 3. Can you think of modern-day mammals that may have descended from these early animals?
2. Look at the images of ice age mammals on page 196. What modern-day mammals do these early animals resemble? How did the ice age animals differ from their modern descendents?
3. Which of the four theories about what happened to ice age mammals has the most convincing supporting evidence?
4. Which of the theories do you think needs more evidence? What types of evidence might scientists look for?

Reading Journal

Write a one-page entry about the most likely relationships between humans and Ice Age mammals. How do you think humans interacted with the mammals? Humans hunted mammals, but do you think the mammals killed humans? Did humans travel near the mammals? Use information from Selections 1, 2, and 3 and your own knowledge to explain.

Learning Vocabulary

EXERCISE 25 Reviewing academic vocabulary

Work with a partner to test each other on the academic words in Selection 3. Each of you should take one of the lists below: List A and List B. Study the sentences in your list. Use a dictionary to look up unfamiliar words. Do not look up unfamiliar words in the other list.

Ask your partner to write answers to each question in your list in complete sentences. The answers should show that he or she understands the bold-faced word. Then, let your partner test you on the other list. Discuss your answers.

List A

1. Name one **species** of Ice Age mammal.
2. Many large mammals disappeared after the Ice Age. Explain this sentence: Scientists have many **theories** about why this happened.
3. What is one **factor** scientists could study about early animals?
4. What do you think Ice Age humans **consumed**?
5. How do you think archaeologists **obtain** information about the age of human and animal remains?
6. What **dramatic** climate change occurred in the Ice Age?
7. What does it mean to "**maintain**" that a theory is true?
8. Why can we say the mystery about the mammals is **ongoing**?

List B

1. What does it mean if the evidence to support a theory is "**conclusive**"?
2. An archaeologist uncovers an early human bone. In an article, she reports the **precise** age of the human based on mass spectrometry testing. How accurate is her calculation about the person's age?
3. Evidence can **demonstrate** that a theory is correct. This means that the evidence does what?

4. If geologists give a **potential** reason for why the Ice Age occurred, does this mean they are certain about the cause? What do they know?
5. Scientists want to discover the **mechanisms** that might have caused the Ice Age mammals to disappear. What are they looking for?
6. Do scientists in the "Combination School" believe there is a **sole** reason for the early mammals' extinction? What do they believe?
7. Scientists believe that humans and animals **coevolved** during the Ice Age. What does this statement mean?
8. How do you imagine Ice Age humans **adjusted** to the climate?

POWER GRAMMAR

Recognizing Word Roots

In Chapter 3, you studied common suffixes (endings) of adjectives. Another important part of words is the *root*. For example, the word *incorrect* consists of the prefix (beginning part) *in* + the root *cor* + the suffix *rect*; the three parts mean "not + totally + right." You can see that knowing the meaning of common roots of words can expand your vocabulary. Study the roots and meanings in the chart.

Root	Meaning	Example words
ology	study of something	anthropology psychology
mamma (*mamm*)	milk-producing organ of female animals	mammogram mammography
mega (*magna*, *macro*)	large, great, huge in size or extent	major megabyte
cede (*cess, ceed*)	to go; stop, give up	ancestor exceed
tend (*tens, tent*)	to stretch, move, be tight, be pulled	extend intense
tain (*ten*)	hold, hold on, keep going	contain contents

EXERCISE 26 Identifying word roots

Identify and define the common roots in the bold-faced words. For each word, write its root(s) and definition of the root(s) on the lines. Check your answers with the chart and a dictionary.

1. In North America the ice sheets developed over an area that **extends** as far south as where the Ohio and Mississippi rivers meet and eastward to central Long Island. The ice sheets advanced and **receded** four **major** times during the million-year period as the climate changed from cold to warm and back again.

   extends   Root(s) _____

                  Definition _____

   receded   Root(s) _____

                  Definition _____

   major   Root(s) _____

                  Definition _____

2. The curator of the Department of **Mammalogy** at the American Museum of Natural History in New York, Dr. Ross MacPhee **maintains** that many "**mega-mammal**" extinctions in the past 40,000 years may have been caused by diseases introduced by humans or animals that traveled with them.

   mammalogy   Root(s) _____

                     Definition _____

   maintains   Root(s) _____

                     Definition _____

   "mega-mammal"   Root(s) _____

                     Definition _____

✔ Assessing Your Learning at the End of a Chapter
Revisiting Chapter Objectives

Return to the first page of this chapter. Think about the chapter objectives. Put a check mark next to the ones you feel secure about. Review material in the chapter you still need to work on. When you are ready, answer the chapter review questions below.

✔ Practicing for a Chapter Test

EXERCISE 27   Reviewing comprehension

Check your comprehension of main concepts, or ideas, in this chapter by answering the following chapter review questions. First, write notes to answer the questions <u>without</u> looking back at the readings. Then, use the readings to check your answers and revise them, if necessary. Write your final answers in <u>complete sentences</u> on separate paper.

1.   When did the most recent ice age begin and end?
2.   During each ice age, what happens to the large ice sheets that cover the land?
3.   What are the <u>five</u> major hypotheses that suggest why the Ice Age occurred?
4.   How did Ice Age humans travel from continent to continent?
5.   Where did the ancestors of the natives of North and South America come from?
6.   Are scientists certain when the first humans arrived in North and South America? When do they think they arrived?
7.   According to archaeologists, where did Ice Age land bridges exist?
8.   What are three main theories about why Ice Age mammals became extinct?
9.   About how many species of mammals disappeared at this time?
10.   What is one piece of evidence that supports the theory that climate caused the mammals to die?
11.   What is one reason why some scientists do <u>not</u> think that humans were solely responsible for the extinctions?

EXERCISE 28   Reviewing academic vocabulary

Here are some of the academic words you studied in Chapter 5. In the chart on the next page, check the box that describes your knowledge of each word. Review the words that are less familiar to you.

Academic word	I think I know what this word means.	I know this word.	I know this word so well that I can use it in a sentence.
hypothesis			
evidence			
interval			
periodically			
modify			
migrate			
site			
factor			
dramatically			
species			
obtain			
conclusive			
precise			
potential			
mechanism			
evolve			
structure			
furthermore			

For each word you checked the box "I can use it in a sentence," write a sentence using the word. Compare your sentences with those of your study group members. Discuss the words you are less familiar with. Add less familiar words and sentences using the words to the vocabulary list in your notebook.

Focusing on Geology and Archaeology

EXERCISE 29 Viewing educational programs and films

Educational television programs and films bring academic subjects to life. They can help you visually understand important concepts you have studied and can expand your knowledge even further.

Assignment

View an educational television program or film about a topic in geology, archaeology, or other related field of science. Then, write a one-page summary and reaction about the film.

Summary and reaction

In your summary and reaction, answer these questions: What is the title of the film? What is it about? If the film presents a theory or hypothesis, what question or questions are scientists trying to answer? What evidence do they give? What are scientists studying in the film? What did you learn from the film? Did you find the film interesting? Why or why not?

Possible film topics, sources, television channels, and film titles

Public Broadcasting Service (PBS) channel
Cracking the Ice Age (NOVA series)
Ancient Creatures of the Deep (NOVA series)
Lost Treasures of Tibet (NOVA series)
Sultan's Lost Treasure (NOVA series)
The Dinosaurs
Ape Man
Journey of Man

The Discovery Channel
Land of the Mammoth

The National Geographic Channel
   Arctic Kingdom: Life at the Edge
   Egypt Eternal: The Quest for Lost Tombs
   Inca Mummies: Secrets of a Lost World

The History Channel/Arts & Entertainment (A&E)
Channel/Biography Channel
   Running Out of Time (extinction of African cheetah and
   rhinoceros)
   NOAHS: Keepers of the Ark (endangered species)
   Charles Darwin: Evolution's Voice

Libraries or video stores

The public or school library and video stores may have the films
listed above and others on subjects in geology, archaeology, or another
related scientific field like biology or anthropology.

WEB POWER

Go to **elt.heinle.com/collegereading** to view more
readings on the Ice Age plus exercises that will help
you study the Web readings and the academic
words in this chapter.

Up from Slavery

ACADEMIC FOCUS: HISTORY

An American Slave Market (1852)

Academic Reading Objectives

After completing this chapter,
you should be able to:

✓ Check here as you
master each objective.

1. Know more vocabulary words used in
   your academic studies ☐
2. Ask questions before you read to prepare
   your mind for reading ☐
3. Distinguish facts from opinions in reading ☐
4. Recognize and use common noun endings ☐
5. Perform better on a multiple-choice test ☐

History Objectives

1. Create a timeline to record important dates
   and events in a reading ☐
2. Read and identify the main parts of a map ☐
3. Pass a multiple-choice test on the content
   of the chapter readings ☐
4. Read primary sources to learn more about
   historical events ☐

Introducing Chapter Themes

▷ Getting Ready to Read

EXERCISE 1 Discussing questions

Discuss the following questions with your classmates:

1. Look at the photograph on page 210. Who do you see? What are the people doing?
2. Did slavery exist in the country in which you were born? Share what you know about past slavery in your birth country.
3. Does slavery exist today? Share your knowledge about slavery across the globe today.
4. For what reasons do you think people enslave others?

STRATEGY

Asking Questions before You Read

Asking questions about a reading's content before you read helps you focus, or concentrate, on the content of your reading. When you ask questions about a reading beforehand, you will look for specific answers to your questions as you are reading.

EXERCISE 2 Reading titles and previewing information

Read the titles of the reading selections below. Think about the selections you will read.

Selections

1. "Slavery in America"
2. "A Slave's Journey in Sudan"
3. "From *Restavec: From Haitian Slave Child to Middle-Class American*"

Ask and answer questions based on the reading titles. Follow these steps:

1. Use the title of Selection 1 to make up questions about U.S. slavery. With a partner, ask each other the questions. Guess the answers to the questions.

   Examples: Who was enslaved in America?

   When did slavery exist in the United States?

   What happened to end slavery?

2. All three selections describe the lives of slaves. Predict ideas in the readings by discussing these questions: What types of work do you think slaves did? How do you think they were treated? What rights do you think slaves had?

3. Selection 2 describes slavery in present-day Sudan. Ask and answer questions using words from the title of this reading selection.

   Examples: Where is Sudan?

   Why is there slavery in Sudan?

4. Selection 2 is also an *editorial*, a newspaper article that gives the writer's opinion. What do you think the writer's views about slavery might be?

5. Selection 3 presents the autobiography of Jean-Robert Cadet, a former *restavec*, or slave, in Haiti. Ask and answer questions using words from the title of this reading selection.

   Examples: How did Cadet become a middle-class American?

   What is a *restavec*?

   Why was a child enslaved?

Reading Assignment 1

▷ Reading for a Purpose

Focusing on History: Timelines

When you read history textbooks, you will find many dates and details. Thinking about events in the form of a timeline can help you understand and remember main ideas. A *timeline* is a type of graphic organizer that shows dates and events in the order in which they happened.

Many history textbooks include timelines. Timelines often appear at the beginning of each chapter. In that way, they provide a quick, "at a glance" preview of the main events that will be presented in the chapter.

EXERCISE 3 Identifying dates and events

Preview the timeline below before you read. As you read Selection 1, look for dates and events. After you read, you will write information about important dates and events on a similar timeline.

Time Line—Slavery in the U.S.

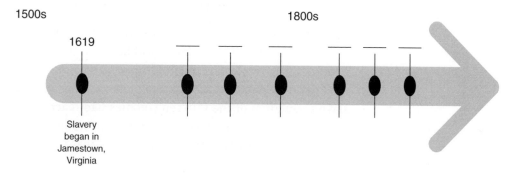

▷ Reading for Information

*As you did with previous readings, read Selection 1, "Slavery in America,"
nonstop without a dictionary. When you read the selection again, use a
dictionary to look up unfamiliar words. Write their definitions in the reading
margins. Annotate important ideas in the text by highlighting or
underlining them.*

Africans on a slave ship bound for America

Reading Selection 1

SLAVERY IN AMERICA

By Dennis Brindell Fradin

1   Nearly fifteen million Africans were kidnapped and sent to
various places in the New World between the 1500s and the
1800s. Slavery began in England's American colonies[1] in 1619 with
the arrival of about twenty black people in Jamestown, Virginia. The
slave population of the thirteen colonies had reached 500,000 by
1776. On July 4 of that year, the American colonists adopted[2] the
Declaration of Independence,[3] announcing that the thirteen colonies

1. *American colonies* = Until 1781, the American colonies were owned by Great
   Britain and controlled from Great Britain.
2. *adopted* = approved officially
3. *Declaration of Independence* = formal written announcement that the United
   States was officially independent from Great Britain

had become the United States. Although the Declaration asserted that "all men are created equal" and are entitled to "Life, Liberty, and the pursuit of Happiness," all thirteen of the new states permitted slavery and excluded slaves from these basic freedoms.

2   In 1780, Massachusetts became the first state to outlaw[4] slavery. Other northern states followed, until slavery was ended in the North[5] by the mid-1800s. Southern planters kept adding to their slave holdings, however, especially after the invention of the cotton gin[6] in 1793 made cotton a huge moneymaking crop.[7] By 1850, there were 3.2 million slaves in the South—one seventh of the nation's population. Many of the slaves grew "King Cotton," but some were house slaves, while others with special skills such as carpentry or haircutting worked in town, earning large sums of money for their owners.

3   Slave life was so harsh it is difficult to imagine. Picture working in a cotton, tobacco, or rice field sixteen hours a day; being whipped by an overseer if you fall behind in your work; eating only old corn and bacon; wearing your only set of clothes day after day; possessing nothing of your own, often not even a last name; having no more rights than a horse or a cow, so that your master can kill you or rape your mother and sisters if he wants; watching helplessly as your relatives are sold to different owners, never to see one another again; being forbidden to learn to read and write; having to show a pass[8] to every white person you meet when away from home; and praying in the "Negro section" of the church, where the white preacher says you will go to hell, should you defy[9] your master or run away. Finally, imagine that if you are caught trying to escape, you may be burned with a red-hot iron, whipped nearly to death, or burned to death. If you can imagine all that, you may begin to have some idea of what slavery was like.

4. *outlaw* = to declare something illegal
5. *the North* = the northern U.S. states during the Civil War, where slavery was later prohibited
6. *cotton gin* = a machine that separates the cotton fibers from the cotton plant's seeds and outer parts
7. *crop* = farm plants or plant products such as grain, fruit, and vegetables
8. *pass* = an official document giving somebody the right to enter a place or to travel freely
9. *defy* = to openly refuse to obey someone or something

4   The story of the slaves who fled in quest of liberty is one of the most exciting chapters in all of history. Making their way through forests, the fugitives usually traveled at night, guided by the North Star. Often they were helped along by the Underground Railroad, a network of hiding places established by abolitionists,[10] where runaways could eat and rest on their trip northward.

5   To this day, many American families speak with pride of ancestors who fled[11] slavery or who hid runaway slaves in their homes. Few of these stories have been written down, however. Not having been taught to read and write, the fugitives[12] were generally unable to record their experiences.

6   Fortunately, a small number of fugitive slave narratives were put in writing. After going to school, several escaped slaves wrote about their experiences, often using false names to make it more difficult for their former owners to locate them. Then in 1865 the North defeated the South in the Civil War,[13] ending slavery forever in the United States. With no fear of being returned to slavery, more ex-slaves wrote about their escapes.

10. *abolitionists* = people who wanted to *abolish*, or end, slavery
11. *fled* = past of *flee*, to run away from trouble or danger
12. *fugitives* = people who run away to avoid being caught
13. *Civil War* = a war in which opposing groups in the same country fight each other; the war in the United States between the North and the South from 1861 to 1865

▷ Assessing Your Learning

Focusing on History: Demonstrating Comprehension

EXERCISE 4   Drawing a timeline

On separate paper, draw a timeline similar to the one at the beginning of this chapter. Use it to record important dates and events about the history of U.S. slavery presented in Selection 1. Write the dates in the blank spaces above the timeline. Below the line, briefly write what occurred on that date. The first important date and event are supplied for you in the sample timeline earlier in this chapter.

Compare your timeline with a partner's. Discuss the information on your timelines with the class.

EXERCISE 5   Expressing the main idea

Which of the following sentences best expresses the writer's main idea? Check the best main idea sentence. Compare your answer with another classmate's. Then, discuss the answer with the class.

_____ Slavery began in the American colonies in 1619.

_____ The reading is about slavery in the American colonies.

_____ Slavery existed in the American colonies for more than two hundred years.

_____ Slave life was very difficult.

Next, match each of the sentences above that you did not choose with one of the following descriptions. Put the letter(s) of the sentence next to the appropriate description. Share your answers with classmates.

_____ This sentence is too general. It only tells what the reading is about.

_____ This sentence is too specific. It tells only about one idea in the reading.

EXERCISE **6** **Checking comprehension**

Work with your partner to answer the following questions. Share your answers with the rest of your class.

1. Add more information to your timeline. Trace the growth of slavery in the United States by writing the <u>numbers of slaves</u> under the following years on your timeline:

   1619   1776   1850

2. What was happening to the number of slaves in the South (the southern U.S. states) at the time that slavery ended in the North? Why?

3. Make a list of slaves' difficult conditions that are described in the reading.

4. According to the reading, what did *abolitionists* do?

5. When did slavery end in the United States? What event caused the end of slavery?

STRATEGY

Distinguishing Facts from Opinions

Your ability to distinguish facts from opinions in readings and spoken language is a critical language learning skill. When you read academic texts or listen to lectures, always consider whether the writer or speaker is telling you a *fact* or whether he or she is trying to persuade you with an *opinion*. If you can do this, you can better evaluate the information you receive. Ask yourself: Has the writer proved this idea? Is it really true? Or is it just the writer's opinion? Don't always believe something just because it is printed.

Examine this passage from Selection 2:

> The story of the slaves who fled in quest of liberty is one of the most exciting chapters in all of history. Making their way through forests, the fugitives usually traveled at night, guided by the North Star.

Do these sentences tell about *facts* or *opinions*?

The first sentence relates the writer's *opinion* because he uses the word *exciting* to describe the slave stories. This is his opinion, not a fact. The second sentence states a *fact*, because slave narratives have proved the existence of nighttime flights of fugitive slaves.

EXERCISE **7**   **Distinguishing facts from opinions**

Read these sentences from Selection 1. Mark the statements F (fact), O (opinion), or N (not sure). Discuss your answers with the members of your study group, and then with your entire class.

1. _____ Although the Declaration [of Independence] asserted that "all men are created equal" and are entitled to "Life, Liberty, and the pursuit of Happiness," all thirteen of the new states permitted slavery and excluded slaves from these basic freedoms. (¶ 1)

2. _____ Slave life was so harsh it is difficult to imagine. (¶ 3)

3. _____ Picture . . . having no more rights than a horse or a cow, so that your master can kill you or rape your mother and sisters if he wants; watching helplessly as your relatives are sold to different owners, never to see one another again . . ." (¶ 3)

4. _____ Picture . . . praying in the "Negro section" of the church, where the white preacher says you will go to hell, should you defy your master or run away. (¶ 3)

5. _____ Often they [slaves] were helped along by the Underground Railroad, a network of hiding places established by abolitionists, where runaways could eat and rest on their trip northward. (¶ 4)

6. _____ To this day, many American families speak with pride of ancestors who fled slavery or who hid runaway slaves in their homes. (¶ 5)

7. _____ Fortunately, a number of fugitive slave narratives were put in writing. (¶ 6)

8. _____ Then in 1865 the North defeated the South in the Civil War, ending slavery forever in the United States. (¶ 6)

▷ Questions for Discussion

EXERCISE 8   **Developing group discussion**

Discuss the following questions with your study group members:

1. In paragraph 1, the writer says: "Although the Declaration asserted that 'all men are created equal' and are entitled to 'Life, Liberty, and the pursuit of Happiness,' all thirteen of the new states permitted slavery and excluded slaves from these basic freedoms." Why does the writer include this information? What point is he trying to make?
2. Reread paragraph 3 of Selection 1. Which of the conditions of slaves do you think was the most terrible? Why?
3. In paragraph 4, the writer says runaway slaves "traveled at night, guided by the North Star." Where were the slaves going? Why?
4. This paragraph also says that the slaves were helped by the Underground Railroad. Why do you think this "network of hiding places" was called the Underground Railroad?
5. What types of people do you think helped slaves escape?

▷ Reading Journal

Write a one-page journal entry about slavery. Choose <u>one</u> of the topics below:

1. Some Americans call the slavery period the most dishonorable time in U.S. history. They feel ashamed because even U.S. presidents owned slaves. Do you agree that the slavery period was the most shameful event in U.S. history? Do you think that other periods have been more disgraceful? Explain.
2. In other parts of the world and at other time periods in history, slavery has existed. Write about slavery in a country other than the United States. (You can write about past or present-day slavery.) Explain when the slavery existed (or exists) and which group enslaved another group. Describe the conditions of slaves and the reasons for the slavery (if you know them).

Use information from Selection 1 and your own knowledge to explain your ideas.

▷ Learning Vocabulary

EXERCISE 9 Guessing meanings from context clues

Study the bold-faced words in the sentences below. Mark the part of speech and/or function above each word. Study the context of the bold-faced word. Return to Selection 1, "Slavery in America," if you would like to reread other sentences that appear before and after the word.

For each bold-faced word in the sentences, choose a synonym or definition from the list in the box. Do not use a dictionary. The first one is done for you.

very large	creation	given the right to have or do something
not allowed	long search	firmly stated an opinion or belief
stories	cruel, hard	people opposed to slavery
force to have sex		

1. (¶ 1) [T]he Declaration **asserted** that "all men are created equal" and are **entitled** to "Life, Liberty, and the pursuit of Happiness," . . .

   <u>*firmly stated an opinion or*</u>   <u>*given the right to have*</u>

   <u>*belief*</u>   <u>*or do something*</u>

2. (¶ 2) Southern planters kept adding to their slave holdings, however, especially after the **invention** of the cotton gin in 1793 made cotton a huge moneymaking **crop**.

   _____   _____

3. (¶ 3) Slave life was so **harsh** it is difficult to imagine.

   _____

4. (¶ 3) Picture . . . having no more rights than a horse or a cow, so that your master can kill you or **rape** your mother and sisters if he wants . . .

   _____

5. (¶ 3) Picture . . . being **forbidden** to learn to read and write.

_____

6. (¶ 5) The story of the slaves who fled in **quest** of liberty is one of the most exciting chapters in all of history.

_____

7. (¶ 5) Often they were helped along by the Underground Railroad, a network of hiding places established by **abolitionists** . . .

_____

8. (¶ 6) Fortunately, a small number of fugitive slave **narratives** were put in writing.

_____

EXERCISE 10 **Defining academic vocabulary**

Scan Selection 1 and look for the five underlined academic vocabulary words printed below with the paragraph number next to each word. Study how each word is used in its sentence.

Match the vocabulary word with the correct meaning from the list on the right. Put the matching letter in the blank space.

1. _____ created (¶ 1)
2. _____ pursuit (¶ 1)
3. _____ sums (¶ 2)
4. _____ network (¶ 4)
5. _____ established (¶ 4)

a. total amounts
b. made something exist
c. started something such as a company, system, etc.
d. a group of people, organizations, etc. that are connected or that work together
e. the act of trying to achieve something in a determined way

Reading Assignment 2

A SLAVE'S JOURNEY IN SUDAN

▽ Getting Ready to Read

Focusing on History: Reading Maps

History textbooks often include maps to show where events occurred. Reading maps well is important because maps often help you "see" the ideas in related reading selections.

Often, the maps also contain information from the readings about the events. To explain this information, a map generally has a *title*, *labels* for places, a measurement *scale* to show distance, and sometimes a *legend* (a brief explanation of markings, colors, or symbols on a map).

EXERCISE 11 **Studying a map**

Selection 2, "A Slave's Journey in Sudan," describes a story of enslavement in the African country of Sudan. As you study the map to the right, find the title, labels, and scale on the map. Be prepared to identify and explain these parts of the map.

Map of Sudan

EXERCISE 12 Checking comprehension

Work with a partner to answer the following questions. Share your answers with the class.

1. What is the capital of Sudan? How is the city marked on the map to show it is the capital?
2. Which countries border Sudan?
3. What body of water is next to Sudan?
4. What are the major rivers in Sudan?
5. From your knowledge and the map, in what part of Africa is Sudan located?

▷ Reading for Information

Read Selection 2, "A Slave's Journey in Sudan," once without a dictionary. Then, use a dictionary to define unfamiliar words. As you read, highlight or underline important ideas for later study.

Dinka slave trade in Sudan

Reading Selection 2

A SLAVE'S JOURNEY IN SUDAN

By Nicholas D. Kristof

1   April 23, 2002, KHARTOUM, Sudan—Abuk Achian was 6 years old when Arab raiders[1] attacked her village in southern Sudan, carried her off on horseback, and turned her into a slave.

2   Ms. Achian, now a pretty woman of 18, is one of many thousands of Sudanese women and children who have been kidnapped and enslaved over the last 20 years. Stopping this slavery will require international pressure.

3   Originally the Sudanese government excused the slave raids, as a way to reward Arab soldiers fighting on the government side in Sudan's civil war. Lately it has begun to crack down on[2] the tribal[3] raiding, although it still tends to deny that slavery exists here.

4   Ms. Achian was one of about 30 former slaves whom I met in Sudan (despite the efforts of the government, which did just about everything it could to limit my reporting here). Her story is typical: She is a member of the Dinka tribe, black Africans who are Christians or animists,[4] while the kidnappers are Baggara, or Muslim Arab herdsmen.[5]

5   "I was so scared," she recalled of her first few weeks in captivity.[6] "I couldn't understand the language that they spoke, and I was crying. But they beat me until I stopped crying and started to learn their language."

6   Her duties were to sleep outside with the camels, milk them, and make sure they did not run off. Her master beat her regularly and prohibited her to ever talk to other Dinka.

---

1. *raiders* = a small group of armed persons who make a sudden, forcible attack
2. *crack down on* = to make an effort to stop bad or illegal behavior by being strict and determined
3. *tribal* = relating to a *tribe*, a group made up of families, clans, or other groups with a common ancestry, culture, and leadership
4. *animists* = persons who believe that individual spirits live in animals and other natural objects
5. *herdsmen* = people whose job is to keep animals of a single kind feeding and moving together in a *herd*, or group
6. *captivity* = the state of being imprisoned, confined, or enslaved

7   Ms. Achian says she tried to escape once. Her master caught her, tied her hands together and lifted her by her arms from a tree branch so that her feet did not touch the ground. Then he beat her into a bloody mess with a camel whip, cut her with a knife and let her hang in the air all night.

8   After a few beatings, she also agreed to become a Muslim. When she was 12, her master sold her to be the bride of a young man.

9   Initially Ms. Achian was afraid of her husband, but soon came to love him and had a son with him.

10   "He treated me well," she said. "He was a very good man."

11   Well, perhaps not that good a man. He too was a slave-raider, and he would periodically go off to attack Dinka villages and return with new slave children. Ms. Achian said she felt sorry for the new slaves but never dared complain to her husband. Then her husband was killed on one of these raids, and Ms. Achian found herself a widow, at age 16. Her parents-in-law seized her son and beat her when she protested, and so she left her boy behind and ran off to freedom.

Source: From "A Slave's Journey in Sudan," by Nicholas D. Kristof, *New York Times*, Editorial Desk, April 23, 2002. Copyright (c) 2002 by The New York Times Co. Reprinted with permission.

▷ Assessing Your Learning

Focusing on History: Demonstrating Comprehension

EXERCISE 13 **Expressing the main idea**

Write one sentence to express the main idea of Selection 2, "A Slave's Journey in Sudan." In your sentence, include the title of the article, the author's name, and the main idea. Compare your sentence with one of your classmate's.

EXERCISE 14 **Checking comprehension**

Work with a partner to answer the following questions. Share your answers with your class. On separate paper, write answers to each question in complete sentences.

1. How was Abuk Achian taken as a slave?
2. According to the writer, who are commonly the enslaved people in Sudan? Who are the slave owners?

3. What were Abuk's duties as a slave?
4. When was she punished?
5. What happened to her at the age of twelve? At the age of sixteen?
6. At the end of her story, what happened to Abuk?

EXERCISE 15 **Writing a summary paragraph**

Write a paragraph-length summary of Selection 2. Begin with the main idea sentence you wrote. This sentence should identify the article by title and author and state the main idea. Continue your summary by presenting the major points in the article—the major events that occurred in the story. Compare your summary with a partner's.

▷ Questions for Discussion

EXERCISE 16 **Discussing the reading**

Discuss the following questions with your study group:

1. In what ways did Abuk's life change after she became a slave?
2. Do you think she handled the changes well? What lines from the story support your opinion?
3. What do you think you might have done in her situation as a young child? As an older child?
4. What is your reaction to what she did at the end of the story?
5. Slavery exists today in several parts of the world. Where does it exist? For what purposes? Share what you know about present-day slavery.

EXERCISE 17 **Writing a reaction response**

Continue the summary paragraph you wrote about Selection 2. Add sentences to express your reaction to the story reported in the article. Use answers to your group discussion questions to help you explain the story events you had strong reactions to. Share your reaction paragraph with your study group.

▷ Learning Vocabulary

EXERCISE 18 Synonyms

For each bold-faced word below, find and circle the synonym or synonyms next to it. Compare your answers with a partner's. The first one is done for you.

1. **Raiders** attacked her village. (thieves) soldiers (bandits)

2. Sudan had a **civil** war. local internal international

3. . . . first few weeks in **captivity** . . . slavery imprisonment bondage

4. . . . **prohibited** from speaking . . . allowed forbidden permitted

5. . . . he would **periodically** go . . . always regularly occasionally

6. . . . **seized** her son . . . captured freed caught

7. . . . beat her when she **protested** . . . cried complained agreed

EXERCISE 19 Studying academic vocabulary

Put a check mark next to the academic vocabulary words from Selections 1 and 2 that you already know.

create(d)	section	civil	periodically
pursuit	network	require	
exclude(d)	establish(ed)	prohibit(ed)	
sum(s)	locate	initially	

Add unfamiliar vocabulary words to your academic vocabulary list. For each word, write a definition and a sentence using the word.

Reading Assignment 3

FROM *RESTAVEC: FROM HAITIAN SLAVE CHILD TO MIDDLE-CLASS AMERICAN*

▽ Getting Ready to Read

EXERCISE 20 Checking comprehension

Selection 3, "From Restavec: From Haitian Slave Child to Middle-Class American," is a story written by a former slave in Haiti. To prepare for reading, study the map above. Then, answer the questions on the next page. Discuss your answers with your classmates.

1. What is the title of the map on page 229? Why does the map have this title?
2. Which country is on the same island as Haiti?
3. Which other large island nations are located near Haiti?
4. Where is Haiti located in relation to the United States? To Central America? To South America?

◹ Focusing on History: Reading Primary Sources

Jean-Robert Cadet, the author of Selection 3, was a *restavec*, or child slave, in Haiti. His book, *Restavec*, may be called a *primary source* because it is a historical account written by the person who experienced it. Reading primary sources gives you a closer, more detailed view of history.

EXERCISE 21 Previewing in group discussion

Discuss the following questions with your study group:

1. In what ways do you think reading this primary source story will give you "a closer view" of slavery?
2. Look back at Selection 1, "Slavery in America," whose author is a writer of history books. What if Selection 1 had been written instead by an American slave? What details (e.g., facts, examples, descriptions) might the story have included? What information in Selection 1 might not have appeared if it had been written by a slave?
3. What information do you think Selection 2, "A Slave's Journey in Sudan," would have included if it had been written by the former slave in the story? What details (e.g., facts, examples, descriptions) might she have added in telling her experiences?
4. The author of Selection 3 says that his story is true but that the names in it were changed. Why do you think he wrote his slave narrative? Why do you think other slaves also wrote their life stories?
5. Imagine this story being told by Florence. How might she have told the story of Cadet coming to live in her home?

▷ Reading for a Purpose

EXERCISE 22   **Asking questions before you read**

Work with your study group to ask questions about the following parts of Cadet's story, briefly summarized below. Write your questions on the lines. Look back at the questions you wrote in Activity 2. Include questions that apply to these parts of the story.

1. Cadet's father gave money to a female friend named Florence and asked her to raise Cadet because his father was already married. Cadet's mother had died.

   _____

   _____

   _____

   _____

   _____

   _____

2. Cadet lived with Florence during his childhood years until Florence immigrated to the United States. Cadet later moved to the United States.

   _____

   _____

   _____

   _____

   _____

   _____

▷ Reading for Information

Read Selection 3 nonstop without a dictionary. Then, use a dictionary to look up unfamiliar words, if necessary. Highlight or underline important parts of the story as you read.

Haitian children

Reading Selection 3

FROM *RESTAVEC: FROM HAITIAN SLAVE CHILD TO MIDDLE-CLASS AMERICAN*

By Jean-Robert Cadet

1 I took a week's vacation and decided to drive to New York to confront[1] Florence. I packed a small bag and took off at three o'clock in the morning. I drove all day, stopping only for food, gas, and rest rooms.

2   The next morning after breakfast, I placed my overnight bag in the car and drove to Florence's house. I parked across the street. The house needed repairs and the yard looked neglected.[2] I walked to the front door with my overnight bag. I knocked. Florence opened the door.

3   "Oh my son, it's you, come in," she said, smiling. She had never referred to me as her son before. "I am glad to see you. I thought you had forgotten all about me," she said. I took a deep breath. I was nervous. "I am not a shoeshine boy," I said. Florence seemed embarrassed. She kept her eyes on the table.

1. *confront* = to come face to face with somebody, especially in conflict
2. *neglected* = not taken care of very well or not given enough attention

4   "I came to tell you how much you've hurt me, but I don't know where to start," I continued with quivering lips. Florence opened her mouth to talk.

5   "Please, don't say anything. It's my turn to talk now. For fifteen years, you prevented me from expressing my wants, my needs, my feelings, and my opinions. You struck me on my eye with the heel of your shoe because I broke a glass. I bled and I could not see with the eye. Look at the scar—I still have it," I said, pointing to the corner of my right eye.

6   "You let your friends borrow me like I was some kind of human vacuum cleaner. Remember when I was supposed to have my First Communion?[3] I received the sacrament[4] in the army. It was embarrassing telling the priest that my mother didn't want to spend money to buy me clothes and shoes." Tears began to flow from her eyes.

7   "You nearly killed me when you put a foot on my neck because I lost a dollar. Yes, I *lost* a dollar. I had a hole in my pocket. You used to give more than that to your lover Paul. Where is he now?"

8   Florence was sobbing.[5] She took a napkin and wiped her eyes.

9   "You stood by and watched as your friend Yvette forced me down on my knees and pushed my head into a dirty toilet. Where is she now? You celebrated your birthday, your son's birthday, your daughter-in-law's birthday, and your grandchildren's birthdays—but every year you said to me that my birthday was last month. Did you really have to lock me out of the house whenever you spent the day with your friends? You could have taken me with you—I was a good boy. A month ago a lady at work put a cake on my desk to celebrate my birthday. You want to know what I did? I took the cake home to my apartment while no one was looking because I did not know what to do. You know, several times I imagined myself killing you." Florence looked up and stared into my eyes.

10   "Why don't you kill me and get it over with right now!" exclaimed Florence.

3. *First Communion* = a Christian ceremony in which young church members for the first time eat holy bread and drink holy wine as signs of Christ's body and blood

4. *sacrament* = same meaning as *communion*, above, but not only for young church members and not necessarily for the first time

5. *sobbing* = crying while breathing in short sudden breaths

11   "I should be here with you to take care of you, to take you out to dinner, and to say proudly to all my friends, 'This is my mother.' But I can't because you hurt me so much." I stood up, still sobbing. I slowly unzipped my bag, pulled out my bachelor's degree, and placed it in front of her.

12   "I am not a shoeshine boy," I said again.

13   I walked out and closed the door behind me, feeling free, renewed, and vindicated.[6] As I approached my car, I took a deep breath and felt as though I was breathing for the very first time.

Source: From *Restavec: From Haitian Slave Child to Middle-Class American*, by Jean-Robert Cadet, 1998. Reprinted with permission of the author.

▷ Assessing Your Learning

Focusing on History: Demonstrating Comprehension

EXERCISE 23   **Expressing your reaction**

Write a few sentences to express your initial reaction to the story told in Selection 3, "From Restavec: From Haitian Slave Child to Middle-Class American." *Share your reactions with your class.*

EXERCISE 24   **Expressing the main idea**

Write one sentence to express the main idea of Selection 3. Compare your sentence with a partner's. Then, share your sentence with your classmates.

EXERCISE 25   **Reconstructing the story**

Work with your partner to complete the following sentences, which recount the story told in Selection 3. Write your sentences on separate paper. When you write, you can use present tense verbs (as shown), or past tense verbs. Share your writing with your study group.

At the beginning of the story, the writer travels to _____.

The writer says that the house he visits looks _____.

6. *vindicated* = proven that someone who had been blamed for something was not guilty

The house he visits belongs to ——————. She is ——————.

Cadet has come there because ——————————————.

He tells Florence that he feels ——————.

He recounts some the terrible things that Florence did to him.

She ————————————————————————.

Florence's friends also treated him badly. One time, ——————.

However, Cadet shows Florence that he has succeeded in his life. He

shows her ——————. He tells her that he is not a ——————. At the

end of his visit, Cadet feels ——————.

EXERCISE 26 **Distinguishing facts from opinions**

Read these sentences from Selection 3. Mark the statements F (fact),
O (opinion), or N (not sure). Discuss your answers with your study group,
and then with your entire class.

1. —————— I drove all day, stopping only for food, gas, and rest rooms. The next morning, I placed my overnight bag in the car and drove to Florence's house. (¶ 1–2)

2. —————— The house needed repairs and the yard looked neglected. (¶ 2)

3. —————— "I came to tell you how much you've hurt me, but I don't know where to start." (¶ 4)

4. —————— "For fifteen years, you prevented me from expressing my wants, my needs, my feelings, and my opinions." (¶ 5)

5. —————— "You struck me on the eye with the heel of your shoe because I broke a glass. I bled and I could not see with the eye. Look at the scar. . . ." (¶ 5)

6. —————— "You let your friends borrow me like I was some kind of human vacuum cleaner." (¶ 6)

7. _____   "Did you really have to lock me out of the house whenever you spent the day with your friends? You could have taken me with you—I was a good boy." (¶ 9)

8. _____   "A month ago a lady at work put a cake on my desk to celebrate my birthday. You want to know what I did? I took the cake home to my apartment while no one was looking because I didn't know what to do." (¶ 9)

▷ Questions for Discussion

EXERCISE 27   **Reviewing with a group**

Discuss the following questions in your study group:

1. The author titled his story *Restavec*, or *slave child*. Why do you think Cadet identifies himself as a slave?
2. When Cadet came to visit Florence, what feelings toward her did he show? Write words below to express how he felt about her.
3. Do you think that Cadet had a right to feel the way he did?
4. Did the writer have a right to say the things he did to Florence?
5. What kind of person do you think the writer is? What clues from the story make you describe him this way?
6. The writer having been enslaved as a child, what kind of life do you think the writer has as an adult? Do you think he has any problems? If so, what kinds of problems?
7. Reread the last sentence of the story: "As I approached my car, I took a deep breath and felt as though I was breathing for the very first time." How did Cadet feel at this moment? In other words, what does he mean when he said he thought he "was breathing for the very first time."
8. Do you think Cadet made the right choice to visit Florence? Why or why not?

▷ Linking Concepts

EXERCISE 28   **Synthesizing ideas from readings**

Discuss the following questions with your study group:

1. Selections 1 and 2 give the reader a picture of the life of a slave. How was the life of a slave in America different from the present-day slavery described in Sudan in Selection 2?
2. In the first two chapter selections, the enslaved people were forced into slavery. How does the story of how Cadet became a slave child differ from the accounts of how people became slaves in the other two selections?
3. In his 1998 book, Cadet identifies himself as a slave. Considering what you have read about slaves in Selections 1 and 2, would you call Cadet a *slave*? If not, what other "title" would you give to identify him and his situation?
4. Which of these three slave situations do you consider to be the worst? Why?

▷ Reading Journal

Write a one-page journal entry about the prevention of slavery. In 1998, Cadet wrote that more than 250,000 restavecs lived in Haiti. He said he hoped the "account of my life inspire[s] nations to protect all their children." What do you think nations can do now to stop slavery where it exists? What could nations have done in the past to stop slavery? Use information from your reading in this chapter, as well as your own knowledge and experience, to explain your ideas.

▽ Learning Vocabulary

EXERCISE 29 **Guessing meanings from context clues**

Use the context clues to help you identify the definition of each bold-faced word in the sentences below. Study the context to determine the word's part of speech or function. Also consider whether the word has a positive or negative meaning. You may want to reread more sentences before and after the sentence printed below. Circle the letter that corresponds to the correct definition.

1. (¶ 4) "I came to tell you how much you've hurt me, but I don't know where to start," I continued with **quivering** lips. Florence opened her mouth to talk.
   a. cold
   b. warm
   c. shaking
   d. calm

2. (¶ 5) "Please, don't say anything. It's my turn to talk now. For fifteen years, you prevented me from **expressing** my wants, my needs, my feelings, and my opinions."
   a. telling
   b. asking
   c. knowing
   d. losing

3. (¶ 5) "You struck me on my eye with the heel of your shoe because I broke a glass. I bled and I could not see with the eye. Look at the **scar**—I still have it," I said, pointing to the corner of my right eye.
   a. bandage
   b. decoration
   c. mirror
   d. mark

4. (¶s 11–13) I slowly unzipped my bag, pulled out my bachelor's degree, and placed it in front of her.
   "I am not a shoeshine boy," I said again.
   I walked out and closed the door behind me, feeling free, renewed, and **vindicated**.
   a. saddened
   b. returned
   c. refreshed
   d. angered again

POWER GRAMMAR

Working with Word Families

As you learned in earlier chapters, words belong to families that consist of words with different forms, or endings. Recognizing endings of each part of speech will help you use the correct form. Common noun endings are underlined in the following words:

Ending	Word	Sentence
-ery, -ory, -ary	slav<u>ery</u>	*Slav<u>ery</u> exists all over the world.*
-ion	popula<u>tion</u>	*The popula<u>tion</u> of U.S. slaves reached 500,000 by 1776.*
-ment	govern<u>ment</u>	*Some govern<u>ment</u>s deny that slavery exists.*
-ence, -ance	independ<u>ence</u>	*The U.S. Declara<u>tion</u> of Independ<u>ence</u> promises*
-ness	happi<u>ness</u>	*that citizens can pursue life, liberty, and happi<u>ness</u>.*
-er, -or	raid<u>ers</u>	*Raid<u>ers</u> captured the girl in her village.*
-ity	captiv<u>ity</u>	*She was held in captiv<u>ity</u> by her capt<u>ors</u>.*
-dom	free<u>dom</u>	*Finally, the girl escaped and regained her free<u>dom</u>.*

EXERCISE 30 **Using noun endings**

Complete the words in the text on the next page with the correct noun endings. In each blank space, add a noun ending from the chart above. Use a dictionary to help you, if necessary. Compare your answers with a classmate's.

AMISTAD

*A*mistad is a film that tells the true story of a group of slaves who overtook a slave ship and won their free_____. The slaves began their journey in Africa. Slave trad_____s captured the slaves and put them aboard a ship, the *Tecoro*. The ship traveled for many months until it reached Cuba. On the way, the slaves lived in terrible condit_____s. When they ran out of food, the sail_____s threw some of the slaves overboard. Finally, the ship reached Cuba. Next, the slave own_____s took the slaves on another ship, the *Amistad*, bound for their plantat_____ nearby. On the *Amistad*, one slave removed his chains and freed the other slaves. The slaves overpowered the sail_____s and told the slave own_____s to sail the ship back to Africa. However, the own_____s tricked the slaves and sailed the ship back to the Americas at night. In the end, the *Amistad* landed on the U.S. coast. The slaves faced imprison_____ again in a U.S. jail. They stood trial for murder. The U.S. govern_____ lawyer tried to prove that the slaves should be returned to captiv_____. Even though the slaves did not speak English, they used hand and facial communicat_____ to tell their story. Then, an African man was found who could translate for the slaves. Finally, they won their case and regained their independ_____. Another ship transported them home to Africa.

▷ Assessing Your Learning at the End of a Chapter

Revisiting Objectives

Return to the first page of this chapter. Think about the chapter objectives. Put a check mark next to the ones you feel secure about. Review material in the chapter you still need to work on. When you are ready, answer the chapter review questions below.

▷ Practicing for a Chapter Test

Master Student Tip

Multiple-Choice Examinations

Multiple-choice examinations are a common type of test at colleges and universities. On multiple-choice tests, the student must choose among several answers, usually labeled *A, B, C, D.* The student may be asked to complete sentences, answer questions, or choose the correct meanings of words. Following some simple techniques will help you perform better on these tests.

EXERCISE 31 **Reviewing for comprehension**

Check your comprehension of main concepts, or ideas, in this chapter by answering the following chapter review questions. First, write notes to answer the questions <u>without</u> looking back at the readings. Then, use the readings to check your answers and revise them, if necessary. Write your final answers in <u>complete sentences</u> on separate paper.

1. What is a *timeline*? Why is it useful when reading historical texts?
2. What are some important pieces of information found in a *map*?
3. Who was enslaved in the United States? Where did these people come from originally?
4. In what ways is a slave's life difficult?
5. When speaking about slavery, what does the term *abolitionist* mean? What does such a person do?

Your instructor will give you a multiple-choice test on the Chapter 6 readings. Here are some tips from the textbook *Becoming a Master Student** to help you perform well on your test:

▶ Step 1: Before the test, study regularly. Study by yourself and with a partner or group. Reread the readings. Discuss the main ideas in the readings. Review the exercises in the chapter. Compare your answers with those of your study partner(s).

▶ Step 2: Ask the instructor. Ask about parts of a reading or about vocabulary words you do not completely understand. Also, ask the instructor what to expect on the test—What topics will be covered? What information are students responsible for learning?

*Adapted from *Becoming a Master Student*, Ninth Edition, by Dave Ellis (2000, Houghton Mifflin Co.)

▶ Step 3: Make a "practice" test. Work with your study partner or group. Divide up the work of making a practice multiple-choice test. For each reading, discuss possible test questions. Write a list of possible questions for each reading. Make up four possible answers for each question. Label the answers *A*, *B*, *C*, and *D*. Test each other on your questions.

Sample Multiple-Choice Test

Directions: Circle the letter next to the best answer for each statement.

1. In America in 1776, ————————————.

    a. there were 500,000 slaves

    b. the American colonies were part of England

    c. the colonists declared their independence

    d. all the above are true.

2. According to "A Slave's Journey in Sudan," slaves ————————.

    a. were stolen from their homes as children

    b. were allowed to speak their native language

    c. were allowed to practice their own religion

    d. were rarely beaten

3. In Selection 3, writer Jean-Robert Cadet shows his "mother" how successful he has become by ————————————.

    a. showing her the money he has earned

    b. giving her many gifts from his bag

    c. showing her his college diploma

    d. giving her a photograph of his family

▶ Step 4: On the day of the test, prepare yourself. Arrive on time to class. Pay attention to the instructor's verbal instructions. Make sure you know how much time you have. Before you begin the test, relax. Take a few deep breaths.

▶ Step 5: Read, read, read! When you get the test, read it over entirely. Quickly think about how much time you have and how many questions you must answer. Notice for how many points each question or section of the test counts. For each part, read the directions slowly. Ask the instructor if you do not understand the directions. Read each question slowly. Reread any parts you are not sure about.

▶ Step 6: Follow these tips when answering multiple-choice questions. If two answers are similar except for one or two words, choose one of these answers. If you have no idea about an answer, guess. Don't leave an answer blank. In general, don't change your answers. Usually your first answer is correct.

EXERCISE 32 Preparing for the test

Follow steps 1 through 4 with the members of your study group. Share your "practice" test with the class.

EXERCISE 33 Using test day techniques

On the day of the test, use the tips in step 4.

EXERCISE 34 Reviewing academic vocabulary

Here are some of the academic words you studied in this chapter. In the chart, check the box that describes your knowledge of each word. Review the words that are less familiar to you.

Academic word	I think I know what this word means.	I know this word.	I know this word so well that I can use it in a sentence.
created			
pursuit			
excluded			
sums			
section			
finally			
chapters			
network			
established			
locate			
civil			
require			
prohibited			
initially			
periodically			

For each word you checked the box "I know this word so well that I can use it in a sentence," write a sentence to use the word. Compare your sentences in your study group. Discuss the words you are less familiar with. Add less familiar words and sentences by adding the words to the vocabulary list in your notebook.

▷ For Further Study

Find a chapter of a book or an article related to slavery. Write a summary paragraph and a reaction paragraph about one or two pages of the reading. As you have learned, a *summary* briefly reports on the main ideas of something you read or heard. A *reaction* piece explains your reaction to or opinion about ideas or information you read or heard.

Steps to Follow

1. Look for a reading on an area of slavery that interests you—for example, slavery in a certain time period or in a certain place.

Possible Sources:

▶ The Internet
Do a search using the key words slavery, slave, *or one of these words plus the name of a country or a date.*

▶ Books
Go to a library and ask a librarian to help you find books about slavery. Use the library's computerized card catalog to help you find a book.

▶ Textbooks
Find a history or political science textbook. Look in the table of contents for readings on slavery.

2. Photocopy a one- or two-page section of the Internet article, book, or textbook. Attach it to a sheet of paper.
3. Under the photocopy, write a paragraph-length summary of the article. In the first sentence, identify the article by title and author name, and include the main idea of the reading. Write additional sentences about the major points and important details in the reading.

4. Then, write a paragraph-length reaction to the ideas in the reading. Use information you learned from reading this chapter or your own knowledge and experience to explain your ideas.
5. Introduce your article and read your summary and reaction paragraphs to your study group.

W E B   P O W E R

Go to **elt.heinle.com/collegereading** to view more readings on slavery, plus exercises that will help you study the Web readings and the academic words in this chapter.

Text Credits